# The Splendour of God

Eric Hammond

**The Splendour of God**

For information and contact visit our website at:
IndoEuropeanPublishing.com

The present edition is a revised version of an earlier publication of this work, produced in the current edition with completely new, easy to read format, and is set and proofread by Alfred Aghajanian for Indo-European Publishing.

Cover Design by Indo-European Design Team

ISBN: 978-1-60444-253-3

**IndoEuropean**
**Publishing.com**
Los Angeles, CA, USA

# CONTENTS

A GLIMPSE THROUGH THE GATE ............................... 1

THE BAB: THE FORETELLER ...................... 8

BAHA'U'LLAH: THE ONE FORETOLD ........................... 13

ABBAS EFFENDI: "THE SERVANT OF GOD" ................... 26

THE SEVEN VALLEYS .............................. 34

TEXTS FROM THE TABLETS ...................... 62

HIDDEN WORDS .................................... 67

# EDITORIAL NOTE

THE object of the Editors of this series is a very definite one. They desire above all things that, in their humble way, these books shall be the ambassadors of good-will and understanding between East and West—the old world of Thought and the new of Action. In this endeavour, and in their own sphere, they are but followers of the highest example in the land. They are confident that a deeper knowledge of the great ideals and lofty philosophy of Oriental thought may help to a revival of that true spirit of Charity which neither despises nor fears the nations of another creed and colour. Finally, in thanking press and public for the very cordial reception given to the "Wisdom of the East" Series, they wish to state that no pains have been spared to secure the best specialists for the treatment of the various subjects at hand.

L. CRANMER-BYNG
S. A. KAPADIA

# A GLIMPSE THROUGH THE GATE

"IN the Beginning was the Word . . . and the Word was Good."

To trace the Word back to the beginning of things, if that were possible, would be to lead back also to the heart of things; to the soul of religion; the light that has illumined all human efforts towards the construction of some external evidence, some symbolic representation, of the spiritual potentiality in mankind.

It is alleged that creeds tend inevitably to ossification; that the vitality of religions is apt to lose itself in their development; that the embroideries of ritual serve, finally, only to obscure the light which they profess to adorn and magnify.

Nothing, throughout history, has been more painfully demonstrated than the barriers to brotherhood built up by the rivalry of religions; a rivalry often more fully emphasised than softened by missionary zeal.

Yet the Source of Spirituality must be one, even as God is one; and the differing languages and systems by means of which spirituality strives to assert itself, although they go far in the direction of perpetuating division between races and men, have, after all, a common origin lying dim and only partially realisable in the shadow of the bygone.

Bahais claim not only the acknowledgment of the spiritual relationship of all men, but its practical endorsement. Visitors to Abbas Effendi, at his home in Acca, are of

1

many tongues and many nations. He has ardent adherents in America, England, France, and Germany, besides thousands of disciples Eastern in education and in temperament. Men of opposing peoples and professions eat at his table together, and the Master himself waits upon his guests in sacred service.

This much has certainly been brought about.

Bahais claim, too, the adhesion of at least a third of the Persian people. They assure us also that the Light, from Acca, has expelled the darkness of division from minds schooled in distrust, if not in hatred, of other minds. More; they claim that Bahaism has, and holds aloft in the light of men, the Light of Love; a light that cannot fail to rend asunder the veil of separation, and enable man to see and love man, notwithstanding any divergence of nation or origin, of colour, caste, or creed.

The shining of this light of love shows man to man as he is, for its rays penetrate the concealing folds of ignorance and suspicion consequent to ignorance.

Wherever Bahais meet they meet on common ground. Throwing aside all the accumulated antagonisms of the past, they rejoice unreservedly in the glad communion of the present; of the day of their Lord.

If Acca, or Rangoon, Paris, London, or New York be their centre of resort, no question of theological theories is permitted to strike a discordant note. Brotherhood, among them, is not merely a "may-be;" it is a visible, actual fact. Buddhist and Mohammedan, Hindu and Zoroastrian, Jew and Christian, sit at one board in amity, eat of one dish, and offer united thanksgiving to one Giver. This most remarkable perception and practice of unity is the result of the light of "The glory of the glory of God."

Illumined by this light, men are no longer blinded by fear of one another; fear is utterly cast out by this light of love.

2

Fear; of violence, of over-reaching, of any evil-doing; fear;—is transformed into fraternity.

The Light "that lighteth every man that cometh into this world," finds its opportunity open. This is the light towards which Bahaism bids all men turn. Luminosity creates love. Before it, darkness and shadows flee away, and doubt, born of darkness, dies. It is the design of Bahaism that men shall not look for evil in one another, but for good. The utterance of Asoka, in his memorable charge to missionaries, is re-uttered by Bahaism to-day:— "'Remember that everywhere you will find some sort of faith and righteousness. See that you foster this, and do not destroy"; and the new utterance is accentuated by inalienable faith in the efficiency of the Light.

In a Talk given by the Master, Abbas Effendi, in Acca, he said:

"Our spiritual perception, our inward sight must be opened, so that we see the signs and traces of God's Spirit in everything. Everything can speak to us of God; everything can reflect to us the Light of the Spirit. When we look at people, we must look at them for the spirit that is in them: we must see them in their relation to God,— that they are His creatures and belonging to Him. We must not look at the faults and imperfections of people, but at the spirit within which causes them to live. Therefore when we look at a man, and love and praise him, the praise is for the signs of God upon him. We must always strive to have a heart clear and pure, so that the Light of the Spirit may be reflected from it in all its fulness."

Differences and distinctions created by creeds are obliterated by the light which shines, glowing and undisturbed, from the one source of all religious impulse and all religious life. Bahaism affirms that all the great

3

prophets and seers, inspirers of great religious movements, were manifestations of the One Divine Light, the One Holy Spirit of God, and that the inspiration is essentially one; notwithstanding divergencies induced by racial or climatic or sacerdotal influence.

The Master, Abbas Effendi, has declared:

"O People! the Doors of the Kingdom are opened; the Sun of Truth is shining upon the world; the Greatest and Most Glorious Light is now manifest to illumine the hearts of men. . . . The Light of Knowledge hath appeared, before which the darkness of every superstitious fancy will be annihilated."

Invited to enquire into the "motif" and the bearing of the Bahais, we are immediately notified that the secret, the impulse, the performance of the underlying principle of unity is indubitably with them. We find in them a consistency, a harmony, commanding reverential consideration. Their attitude towards men of all lands and all languages; their philosophic and practical acceptance of the oneness of real religion, compel our studious recognition.

This pronouncement of Baha'u'llah is as lucid as it is steadfast:

"O ye discerning ones of the people! Verily the words which have descended from the Heaven of the Will of God are the source of Unity and Harmony for the world. Close your eyes to racial differences. Welcome all with the light of oneness. Be the cause of the comfort and the advancement of humanity. This handful of dust, the world, is one home; let it be in unity. Forsake pride: it is a cause of discord. Follow that which leads to harmony."

The spiritual unification of the race is the great aim of

Bahaism. It does not propose the wholesale disintegration of creeds and cults, but, looking through these, discerns the shining of the light, behind, beyond. It recognises the truth in each religious phase, but decries any attempt of any phase to pose as sole interpretation of the truth.

It regards the Kingdom of God as universal rather than particular in the range of its realm. Each prophet, each seer, had his message to deliver, and the burden of that message, rightly interpreted, was "The Lord our God is one God"; not "The Lord our God is for one people."

"These supreme, holy souls" (the prophets or manifestations) "are God-like in their attributes. The garments in which they appear are different, but the attributes are the same. In their real and intrinsic power, they show forth the Perfection of God. The reality of God in them never varies; only the garment in which the Primal Reality is clothed is different according to the time and place of their appearance and declaration to the world. One day it is the garment of Abraham, then Moses, then Jesus, then Baha'u'llah. Knowledge of this oneness is true enlightenment. Some see the garment only and worship the Personality; some see the reality and worship in spirit and in truth. Some of the Hebrews admired the embroidered beauty of the garment of Abraham, but were blind to the Real Light which shone upon the darkness of the world through him. Moses was denied, Jesus was denied, crucified; all have been denied and persecuted for this reason. Men see the garment and are blind to the reality; worship the Personality and do not know the Truth, the Light itself. Some worship the Tree of Life, but do not eat of the blessed Fruit of the Tree. Therefore differences and disagreements arise in religious belief. If all men ate of the Fruit itself, they could never disagree. . . Terms are of no importance. The Fruits of the Tree should be our desire. These are the spiritual 'grapes.' Find the

5

Light itself, and there will be no difference of opinion or belief as to the Personality or Degree of the Manifestations of God."

To Jesus the Christ this question was put by His disciples: "Tell us, What is the Sign of Thy Presence?" Our Lord replied, "As the lightning doth come forth from the East and doth appear unto the West, so shall be also the Presence of the Son of Man." The manifestation that instructs Bahaism to-day says:

"The greatest proof of a manifestation is the Manifestation Himself.

We do not have to prove the existence of the sun. The sun is independent of proof. He who has sight can see the sun and prove it for himself. . . . The sun's light is indispensable. . . .

God with all his qualities is independent of all His creatures. Look at the Christ. He was a youth of Israel, not a great and honoured man, but from a poor family. He was so poor that He was born in a manger; yet He changed the conditions of the whole world. What proof could be greater than this that He was from God? . . .

Without this Light the world could not grow spiritually.

The Blessed Perfection (Baha'u'llah) came from Persia, which is not a prominent nation.

The great Prophets did not enter school to be taught of men; yet so many things did they manifest that at last we must admit that the world is not able to destroy the wisdom of the Prophets or grow without them. . . . How the Truth in Christ spread all over the world! . . . The Light of God will shine, must shine. . . . The Blessed Perfection, during His own lifetime, had one thousand followers who believed in Him. Only one proved ungrateful, yet he did not deny Baha'u'llah. Many were martyred with His Name upon their lips."

Here, in small compass, lies the assumption and the promise of Bahaism; the aspiration of Abbas Effendi of Acca; and the "sure and certain hope" of all those who serve under his standard to-day.

# THE BAB: THE FORETELLER

THREE phases of Bahaism have to be considered.

First, that of *The Bab*; then that of *Baha'u'llah*; lastly that of *Abdul Baha*, usually designated *Abbas Effendi*, the recognised head and heart of Bahaism as it is known to-day.

*The Bab: The Foreteller*

(arose in Shiraz, May 1844. Executed in Tabriz, July 1850).

Sixty-four years have passed since he whom many believers rejoiced in hailing "The Bab," "The Door," began, in Persia, his singular and successful career.

As One said, ages ago, "I am The Way," so Mirza Ali Mohammed said, "I am The Door."

That One also declared that He came "not to destroy, but to fulfil." So came Mirza Ali Mohammed, not attempting in any degree to uproot the teachings and doctrines of the creator of the Koran, but to urge a complete whole-hearted performance of the Prophet's commandments.

"The Bab"—for as such he was acknowledged and will be reverently remembered—believed emphatically this: that, "in the past, whenever there was need, God raised up a Prophet on the earth, bearing a book containing a Divine Revelation; and He will do the same in the future, whenever there is need."

He believed, every whit as emphatically, that he, in his own person, was inspired by God as the Prophet for his time. That belief, that inspiration, compelled him to put implicit confidence in the continuity of God's dealings with mankind; a continuity which, always at requisite intervals, proclaims the Divine Message through prophetic lips. That Message should, practically, be one and the same, though the lips that proclaimed it might employ varying words and languages; might even, perchance, direct seekers after God to pursue apparently antagonistic methods.

The Book of The Bab was entitled "The Bayan," and, taken generally, it constituted a new rendering of much that the Prophet of Islam had written, spoken, and enforced.

Steadfast as his belief in himself was, he believed also, as steadfastly, that, while he held open the Door of the Courtyard of God, another, greater than he, should come after him. He realised, he foretold, the arrival of a later Prophet whose mission must excel his own in the power of its purpose, in its fuller acceptance, in its far wider claims upon the minds of men. For him, Persia was the centre of his action; its regeneration and reformation, his immediate and ultimate desire.

To his successor, the whole world lay open; to be subdued by the strength of the sweetness of the Love of God.

His own gracious pleadings with his own people were not made in vain. Historic records of the rejection of prophecy by the powers that be were enlarged by another, bitter, chapter. The endeavour of Persian people to put into practice, at his instigation, a deeper, nobler conception of religion, was misinterpreted.

The priesthood fought for prestige and privilege; for this fearless lover of the light spoke straight to the hearts of his hearers without priestly intervention or clerical approval.

Where the priests were faulty in their duties or in their

example, The Bab spoke of the love of God and bade men directly worship and obey Him.

Priestcraft, backed by governmental action, accused prophet and people of a design to attempt the overthrow of religion and order. Fear entered into the thought of those who, having and misusing the authority of the State, could not, or would not, comprehend these men who looked and longed for the authority of God.

These latter sought an entrance into heaven; the former suspected them of endeavouring to set up their own will in defiance of the Shah and of Islam.

Discourtesy was followed by abuse; abuse by persecution; persecution by spoliation and execution.

After enduring the confinement of a prison, The Bab was shot to death, publicly, in Tabriz.

During two years The Bab had wrought and taught. The theme of his teaching was always "fitness for God." Purity of life, righteousness of conduct, perfect honesty and honour formed variations of that theme. It was one which, commending itself to those who truly sought to serve and reign with the Creator, caused the pharisaical and the proud to blaspheme against the speaker.

Clerical and constituted authority opposed him vehemently. He was accused—no difficult task in such a country and under such circumstances. Next came imprisonment, lasting four years. Throughout this period, notwithstanding anxiety for his many friends,—impelled partly perhaps by that anxiety; certainly impelled by the inspiration to work for the people while life lasted,—he wrote a large number of epistles and exhortations.

His care for his flock concerned their daily doings as well as their eternal welfare. He was literally their "Father in God," taking into account all their environment and all their difficulties and directing them so to live in this world as to prepare themselves fully for the endless life to come.

Some of the epistles reached one country and some another; and while their author was in prison for conscience' sake, his words made their way far and wide. Readers of most lands had, even then, known something of the work of this earnest and devoted reformer.

His institution of a "group" did much to strengthen and enlarge his influence. It comprised eighteen of his earliest disciples. He described them—including himself as "The Point"—"The Nineteen Letters of the Living." These chosen persons were carefully instructed how to instruct others, and how to control and advance the reform of soul and of conduct which The Bab endeavoured to induce among his beloved Persians. He especially bade these eighteen to prepare the way for, and be always ready to receive, One who was about to appear; One whom God would "make manifest." The time of the coming of this Appointed One was given. That He should surely come, The Bab never doubted at all. When He came, He could not fail to be recognised as a "Great Teacher," who would "show signs of divine power and strength"; more, "through His teachings the divine unity of mankind would be established."

Scarcely, perhaps, can too much stress be laid on The Bab's insistence upon the coming of One who should open up and augment the way and the end of his pious design.

The Bab's own personal message was, so to speak, intended for the immediate requirements of his time. The Light that should enlighten not only Persians but the sons of men generally, would inaugurate a new order of things, regenerating all.

Anticipating this Arrival, The Bab endured, wrote, and taught, until his accusers charged him with heresy.

Confiscation of property was, as might have been expected

11

of the persecutors of that country and period, remarkable for its thoroughness. Poverty, want, sickness, were patiently and uncomplainingly borne. After enduring the strain and confinement of a prison, The Bab was shot to death, publicly, in Tabriz, in July 1850. Imprisonment and martyrdom of The Bab were followed up by a wholesale raid upon his followers. We are told that "over twenty thousand of these willingly gave up their property, families, and lives, rather than recant their faith."

The extraordinary personality and influence of The Bab cannot be gainsaid. His spirituality; his contempt for worldly and material things; his masterful grasp of religious and philosophical points; his vast love for and understanding of the people and their deepest needs; all these substantiated his position and supported his claim.

He had exhorted his pupils to "endure all" for the sake of God and their faith and his.

They obeyed. They went to prison rejoicing in the certain triumph of the truth that they adored; the truth that freed them from the fetters of the world. Torture could not wring expressions of regret from their parched but smiling lips.

Life, eternal life, fulness of joy in the perpetual presence of God, had been promised; and, in the conviction that that glorious certainty must be fulfilled in their own experience, they trampled fear of death under foot. Death had, for them, verily lost its sting. This not for a little time, but for year after year. Indeed it is noted that these persecutions continued down to the beginning of the new century.

In 1901 "there were one hundred and seventy martyrs at one time in the city of Yeza." [1]

---

[1] "Their spirit of self-devotion and love is well exemplified in the manner in which Mirza Kurban Ali, one of seven executed together in

# BAHA'U'LLAH: THE ONE FORETOLD

CHRISTIANS were first so called at Antioch.

Bahaism received its earliest momentous impulse at Adrianople. Mention of "over twenty thousand" leads to the supposition that the followers of The Bab had attained to a notable number as well as finality of decision. His views had been disseminated throughout Persia, and, to an appreciable extent, beyond its boundaries.

Preachers of the new form of the old faith travelled far afield, undeterred by suspicion or surveillance, and, in their journeying, sowed the seeds of belief in many comforted hearts.

One or other of these preachers had been heard with avidity by a youth of high lineage—Mirza Hussein Ali—who, drawn by the grace and perfection of the message, became not only a willing adherent, but a zealous and powerful advocate. All the energy he possessed bodily, mental, spiritual—he threw into the service of God and of The Bab.

---

Teheran in September 1850, met his death. When he was brought to the foot of the execution-pole, the headsman raised his sword and smote him from behind. The blow only wounded the old man's neck and cast his turban upon the ground. He raised his head and exclaimed: 'Oh, happy that intoxicated lover who, at the foot of his Beloved, knoweth not whether it be his head or his turban which he casteth.'"—PROFESSOR E. G. BROWNE, *A Traveller's Narrative*.

Persian by birth and breeding, a native of Teheran, he came, there, into this world in 1817, his father, we learn, being a Vizier, his grandfather Grand Vizier. An aristocrat among aristocrats, he knew little or nothing of the education of Scribes or the philosophies of Pharisees. Born in the rank of those who ruled, he had neither opportunity to seek the learning of the schools nor desire to cope on equal terms with the Mullahs, with Mohammedan specialists. To pose as a priest-in-ordinary was out of his power. The lore of the sacerdotalist was outside the scope of his station. Unable to rely on knowledge acquired by man, he had, perforce, to trust implicitly to inspiration, and inspiration supported him to a marvel.

He was something short of thirty when he attached himself to the Babis and became their unfaltering teacher and leader.

Like Francis of Assisi, he chose poverty and vilification with the followers of the faith above the state and luxury of his peers in high places. Like Paul of Tarsus, he "preferred affliction with the people of God." Like Gautama the Buddha, he, quietly yet gloriously, shared in the Great Renunciation. Like the Hebrew Psalmodist, he might have sung, "I had rather be a doorkeeper in the House of my God, than dwell in the tents of wickedness."

He speedily acquired a position of admiration and reverence. His kindly, straightforward character, his profound devotion to The Bab and his principles, were appreciated long before he declared himself to be The One whom, according to his predecessor, "God would make manifest,"

The persecution and martyrdom of The Bab, and the persistent maltreatment of the Babis, resulted in an even closer clinging to the Prophet's revelations. This, again, seems strictly in accordance with the history of religion. "The blood of the martyrs is the seed of the Church."

It must be recorded that his message and his mission were alike peaceful.

No element of antagonism to rule or ruler found place in his scheme of things; for that scheme, being based on spirituality, and working entirely on the spiritual plane, had no space in it for the upsetting of recognised authority. It aimed at persuasion; it condemned coercion.

The central design of Baha'u'llah was peace: peace internal, external, universal; and such peace, he knew, could not in any wise become an accomplished fact unless it were the flower of the soul resulting in the fruition of Divine Love.

We must note, too, in this connection, that The Bab had specifically prophesied the advent of One whose words and wisdom would substantiate his position as Godhead made manifest. His character would be akin to The Light of the world; radiating, penetrating, informing; spreading near and far the beams of a Sun of Righteousness.

As we have seen, no seeds of discord were cast, on the political field; but, in this drama of the incoming of a novel representation of eternal faith, insinuation and denunciation had play and place. No violent outcry against the powers that be had any part in Baha'u'llah's project of peace. We are forced to record the fact that these powers could not, or would not, bear the advent of The Light. In agreement with historic precedent, persecution followed—fierce, fanatic, almost inhumanly cruel.

Imprisonment, confiscation, and torture served to impart firmer faith. Within a year of The Bab's unrighteous execution, a number of his people were confined, Baha'u'llah among them.

Teheran, which bore him in a palace, put her noblest born in prison. He was kept in chains and his wealth

15

appropriated. Family estates, vast and remunerative (there were, we learn, no fewer than five of these), were annexed "by authority." Finally he, with his friends, became exiled to Baghdad.

Still he taught; still his influence increased; still greater affection and devotion centred around him.

Retreat into the wilderness; passing apart to pray; retirement from men, in order that the Vision of God may be apprehended has any Prophet or Seer prophesied or seen without this?

Baha'u'llah spent two years alone among the mountains hard by Baghdad, praying, meditating, dwelling there with God.

After this came the time of the proclamation.

His declaration of Himself as the fulfilment of the Foreteller's prophecy, the "Manifestation of God," was apparently, at first, made at a period of anxiety and distress, to a few of the elect.

The public proclamation did not occur for four or five years, when, being uttered, it was forthwith accepted by the great majority of the Babis, The Bab's adherents, as of divine origin. Baha'u'llah was now the generally recognised chief of the movement. Disciples formerly calling themselves "Babis," adopted the title "Bahais."

The main motive of Baha'u'llah's mission was that of "establishing peace and religious unity [2] in the world."

---

[2] "He called to men of every creed and race to come under the standard of Unity which he had upraised, and assist him in establishing the Kingdom of God and the Brotherhood of Man upon the earth."—S. SPRAGUE.

Baha'u'llah "declared Himself" in 1863. Having journeyed with them to Baghdad, we must accompany him and his people farther still. Fear took hold upon the Mohammedan Mullahs; unfeigned fear of the Prophet's predominance. Were all in the land living in love and peace and unity, what might become of the priestly power and purse? The Mullahs sent to Constantinople for official interference and assistance, and their petition was answered. The Bahais were summoned to the capital.

Banishment to Adrianople—so ran the unalterable decree. To Adrianople our persecuted religionists were bidden.

During his residence there, Baha'u'llah found time to address the Pope and the monarchs of Europe in epistles urging the establishment of unity, the abandonment of injustice, and the abolition of warlike practices. Adrianople was not permitted to contain him long. He and his friends were finally sentenced to exile at Acca (Acre) in Syria, actually a penal colony north of Mount Carmel, [3] a place dreaded for its pestilential atmosphere and its inaccessibility. The thought that fever might speedily attack and slay the Prophet bred a hopeful joy in his persecutors' minds. They arranged, with considerable cruelty, that "the faithful few" should exist as best they could in a couple of rooms in the barracks of the town. There were some seventy confined so for two years.

The indictment leading to this severity comprised many misdemeanours. These God-fearing, God-seeking souls were accused as murderers and thieves. They were branded as Nihilists. [4] Liberty, freedom of any sort, was forbidden them. Of a truth they "endured hardships, as

---

[3] "Here in the land of Zion and Carmel, where 'the coming' in this latter day has been told of all the prophets, Baha'u'llah lived and taught, many travelling from great distances to hear him, while others received teaching from his writings."—C. M. RÉMEY.

[4] "The charge to the Governor stated that they were . . . Nihilists."— ETHEL J. ROSENBERG.

17

good soldiers" of the Cause that was, for them, far more captivating than bodily captivity; they still rejoiced in the Light that led.

Among the seventy suffered Baha'u'llah's brother, to whom death brought release. Such was the insecurity of the roof of the place that, while he sought purer air than that of the room below, and greater quiet for reflection on "the things of God," it gave way. He who prayed fell through the roof, and so died. Despite the close confinement, the absence of any comfort, the unhealthiness of their condition, the prisoners conducted themselves with unfailing courtesy and gentleness. They found grace in the eyes of the governor of their gaol, who, probably touched by the death of his brother, gave Baha'u'llah leave to hire a house within the town. Even here he was obliged "to live and move and have his being" in one apartment only, and this for seven years. One governor left, another came. Each, before his term expired, or, for some end, he was withdrawn, learned that respect and reverence were due to these kindly, uncomplaining folk. A most welcome extension of privileges came with later years, and the Prophet, at length, found himself allowed to wander "within a radius of eighteen miles."

So, "persecuted but not forsaken," Baha'u'llah dwelt on sacred soil, working on, teaching on, never dreaming of despair. Captivity lasting forty years had, surely, weakened if not destroyed both hope and faith in an ordinary mind. Equally surely, the strengthening and growth of hope and faith with each year as it came and went, furnishes emphatic testimony to Baha'u'llah's claim that his spiritual support and sustenance were divine. He remained mentally vigorous until, in 1892, when seventy-five years old, he was called to the nearer Light.

It is at least an interesting coincidence, that from the very quarter of the East from which "A Great Light" shone twenty centuries ago, Baha'u'llah should have been compelled to dwell; "Baha'u'llah"—"The Glory of God"—and that thence his Light should have also shone, illuminating Jew and Gentile, Moslem and infidel. Here, at Acca, he who at Teheran was for his goodness and benevolence called "The Father of the Poor," possessed his soul in patience, in poverty and degradation; yet lived to dispense the Light. Imprisonment and ignominy failed to darken the rays that penetrated far beyond the walls of Acca. That obscure town, by sheltering the Prophet, became the Lantern of the Light.

By word and pen he had prepared men for the reception of illumination. He wrote "tablets" to friends and enquirers at home and abroad, abundantly explaining the why and the wherefore of his mission on earth.

He did not profess the creation of a new creed or to plant the roots of a new religion. On the contrary, he taught that all religions sprang from the Divine Root. He desired rather to revoice the utterance of those divinely appointed ones on whose words and authority the religions of the world were based. This new utterance was indispensable to the welfare of the world; for people had become careless and given over to laxity of thought and life. Every man was bidden to remain in affiance with that form of faith in which he found himself, but to break through the encrustations that had hidden its power and beauty. The true spirit of the founder of the faith would then again become recognised, and the believer was urged to follow and obey that spirit in sincerity. The truth had, so Baha'u'llah taught, been revealed by those Inspired Ones after whom the great religious bodies were named. These had appeared at different historic stages, in diverse places, during various eras in the progress of humanity, but the essence of their message had been one and the same. Its expression only had differed, in order to accommodate it to the requirements of time and place.

Baha'u'llah's gracious persistence in this inner truth, the life-giving element in every religion worthy of the name, had a notably unifying effect upon those who heard, and, hearing, saw. Their attitude towards one another, when they were of differing outward belief, underwent a holy transformation. Men of one creed grasped the hands of those of another creed. Religious fraternity, experienced in the heart, became visibly manifest in the life. The head followed where the heart led. [5]

Under the holy influence of Baha'u'llah, his followers rejoiced in putting the Brotherhood of the race into everyday practice. In all circumstances, whether of kindness or cruelty, of courtesy or of disfavour, the Bahai employed the soft answer that turneth away wrath. Through each chapter of the volume of life the theme of Baha'u'llah's message passes, leaving in its wake the power of his personality, the sweetness of his soul. Swayed by his gospel, Bahais believe in and employ perfect amity towards all men; unswerving toleration towards the perceptions and principles of others than themselves.

Manifold "tablets" and treatises of instruction fell from Baha'u'llah's pen. One treatise, entitled *The Book of Laws*, contains text upon text of commandments invaluable not to Bahais alone but to "all the men of all the world." In it he orders the sword to be set aside for ever, to be replaced by the Word. He inculcates the settlement of national differences by arbitration. He enjoins the acquirement of One Universal Language to be taught to all children in all schools so that "the whole world may become one homeland." Boys and girls are to be educated alike, and the education must be the best possible, participated in by the children of the poor as well as those of the wealthy.

---

[5] "I found that this faith" (Bahaism) "does not expend itself in beautiful and unfruitful theories, but has a vital and effective power to mould life towards the very highest ideal of human character."—PROFESSOR G. GRANVILLE BROWNE, M.A.

"This spirit of love and service to fellow-men was exemplified in an Indian Bahai actually giving his life to save mine, and 'Greater love hath no man than this,'"—SYDNEY SPRAGUE.

Progress is impossible while ignorance spreads its roots. So eager was he in this connection that he wrote: "He who educates his own son or the son of another, it is as though he educated the Son of God." That "work is prayer" he taught decisively. The highest act of prayer and worship consists in the acquirement of some profession or handicraft and using it thoroughly and conscientiously. By the advancement of art and science he set great store. Disapproving of celibacy, he advocated marriage. Objecting to asceticism, he advised his followers to mix freely with all people, and on all occasions to exhibit signs of a glad and joyous but practically righteous life. Naturally, therefore, intemperance and gambling are forbidden, together with the use of opium. Naturally, also, questions of hygienic and sanitary sort receive all possible attention and use.

Practical charity, practical goodwill and kindness to all and sundry, including the lower animal world, Baha'u'llah insisted upon.

History has a perhaps unwholesome habit of repeating itself. Religions in the past were instituted, religious reformations realised, by devout men divinely inspired, who, certain of the source of their inspiration, refused worship themselves in any form. More; they definitely, in remarkable instances, forbade such worship while they dwelt on earth or after their departure in body from the world. Announcements to the effect that "I am of Paul" or "I am of Apollos" were interdicted. Temple-building and altar-raising in adoring memory of prophets and preachers set in, usually, nevertheless. Within measurable distance of the prophet's ascension, temples have arisen, worship made compulsory to adhesion.

Baha'u'llah declared himself utterly opposed to priesthood. He built no church "made with hands." Teachers of his Gospel of The Light may not take fees or stipends for their teaching. The necessities of living must be earned by them, even as St. Paul wrought at sail-making for food.

This lofty impression of spiritual practice presents an ideal worthy of profound consideration, of cordial imitation. That it passes beyond the ideal by having been, and being, the rule of life among the Bahais, is an accredited fact.

That this Religion of The Light is the need of the world throughout; that his mission, and that of his successor, was to illumine the dark places of the earth, Baha'u'llah knew. The world awaited him and he had come. The Light, enkindled, must regenerate man. In far-seeing faith, he wrote:

"O Children of Baha! Associate with all the people of the world, with men of all religions, in concord and harmony; in the spirit of perfect joy and fragrance.

Remind them, also, of that which is for the benefit of all; but beware lest ye make the Word of God the cause of opposition and stumbling, or the source of hatred among you.

If ye have a word or an essence among you which another has not, say it to him with the tongue of love and kindness; if it be accepted and impressed, the end is attained; if not, leave him to himself and pray for him, but do not molest him.

The tongue of kindness is attractive to the heart and it is the sword of the spirit; it furnishes the true relation of thought to utterance; it is as the horizon for the arising of the sun of wisdom and knowledge.

Creatures were created through love; let them live in peace and amity."

The Light of Love is the living lamp of Bahaism. No man's

religion may be ridiculed or opposed, but all men must be urged to be that which his religion, at its best and fullest—at the instant of its initiation—bade him to be. Baha'u'llah saw that God is to every human being as great as the individual mental capacity permits one to see Him." Is there, then, any wonder that he prayed, "Open Thou their eyes that all men may see the Light?" Is there any wonder that his faith in the Light was supreme?

Its rays flashed from the torches upheld by the great Prophets of the great creeds. Obscured by veiling accumulations, The Light still shines, and its shining must become visible when veiling curtains are drawn aside.

Distrust of fellow-men; intemperance of speech or action; love of wealth; above all, disunion: these are strenuously disapproved of by Bahaism.

A tablet, revealed by The Blessed Perfection, as his disciples delight to call him, contains these texts:

"In wealth, fear is concealed and peril is hidden.

There is no continuance in the riches of this world; that which is subject to mortality and undergoeth a change, hath never been and is not worth regarding.

As is well known, the purpose of this Oppressed One in enduring these adversities and calamities . . . has been to quench the fire of hatred and animosity, so that, perchance? the horizons of the minds of the people of this world may shine with the light of concord and attain the real tranquillity. . . .

O people of the world! I enjoin ye to that which is the means of the elevation of your station. Hold to the virtue of God and grasp the hem of that which is just.

Verily, I say, the tongue is for mentioning that which is good; pollute it not with evil speech. God hath forgiven ye that which is past; hereafter ye must all speak that which is befitting.

Avoid execration, reviling, and that which is aggravating to man.

The station of man is high.

The station of man is great, if he holds to reality and truth and if he be firm and steadfast in the commands.

The true man appeareth before the Merciful One like unto the heavens; his sight and hearing are the sun and moon; his bright and shining qualities are the stars; his station is the highest one. . . .

O people of the world! The Creed of God is for love and union; make it not to be a cause of discord and disunion. .

He hath forbidden strife and dispute with an absolute prohibition in the Book (Kitba-el-Akdas).

This is the command of God in His greatest manifestation, and He hath preserved it from any order of annulment and hath adorned it with the ornament of confirmation.

Verily, He is the All-knowing and the All- wise. . . .

My Branches! In this Existent Being the greatest strength and the most perfect power is hidden and concealed.

Look towards It and gaze in the direction of Its union, and not at Its seeming differences.

This is the Testament of God, that the Branches, Twigs,

and Relations must each and every one look to the Greatest Branch."

To disarm prejudice by pure piety; to bid men believe in the One Source of the religious idea rather than struggle for a sacerdotal or prohibitive form; to affirm himself as the unveiler of the truth in all creeds, the Bond of Union between all good men who differ because of external ritual; to proclaim the coming of Another through whom the peoples of the world should exist together in harmonious relationship under the banner of perpetual peace; this was the mission of Baha'u'llah.

His mission terminated in 1892.

It remained for his appointed successor to inaugurate another and larger presentation of the principle of Universal Peace and of the Divine Unity which The Bab and Baha 'u lah had preached and prayed for.

# ABDUL BAHA:
# "THE SERVANT OF GOD"

ABBAS EFFENDI

THAT the Bahais should not be left unshepherded was fore-ordained.

Baha'u'llah, with unerring insight, recognised the undoubted fitness of his eldest son for the leadership of his fast-increasing flock.

This son, known now as Abbas Effendi, was born on May 23, 1844; "the day on which The Bab began his ministry." [6]

Not only had he eagerly assimilated the instructions of The Bab; he had also perceived and rejoiced in the fulfilment, in his Father's person, of The Bab's prophecy that "God would become Manifest."

His acquiescence in, and joyous acceptance of Baha'u'llah was complete. He called him "Lord" as well as "Father."

Used to the existence of the exiled; accustomed to all the details and requirements of the position; filled with unalterable faith in The Bab's message;—his Father's mission;—his own standing as "The Chosen One"; he took upon himself the burdensome yoke, the onerous duties, of "The Servant of God."

---

[6] "From childhood his father fitted him and trained him to become the centre of the movement."—C. M. RÉMEY.

His knowledge of the sufferings of his people was personal and profound; he had shared in their sacrifice. His conviction that, through Bahaism, East and West would be, in God's good time, brought together in the Divine Unity, enabled him to take up bravely the burden imposed upon him by his Father.

Very wisely, as well as very bravely, has he borne that burden.

Abdul Baha, Abbas Effendi, exhibits to perfection the force and sweetness of what we call personality. We have noticed that he addressed his parent sometimes as "Father," sometimes as "Lord." This beautiful appreciation of a beautiful character is repeated in the home of Abbas Effendi, whose daughters employ the same expressions. He who is their Father according to the flesh, is also their Lord according to the spirit. They recognise in him the ideal blending of attributes human and divine; and, in this connection, it must be remembered that it is a man's family who know him most intimately. He who is both loved and reverenced by his own children has a "personality" which survives, and is exalted by, criticism.

Men of various nationalities, rightly proud of intimate acquaintance with him, speak enthusiastically of him as a living example of the practice in everyday life of the highest and, at the same time, most endearing qualities. An Englishwoman, after eight months' residence under his roof, expressed herself as having found her esteem and admiration of Abbas Effendi increase day by day. Known as "The Servant of God," the fitness of that description is proved and recognised by his service to man. His method of life has been, and continues to be, a luminous example of the fact that, here and now, despite all the surroundings of struggle for fame and wealth and material mastery, an existence guided and guarded by the Light of the Spirit is a possible, actual thing. Those who pray for the coming of the Kingdom of God on earth, may see in Abbas Effendi one who dwells in that kingdom consciously, and creates an environment pulsating with the Peace that passeth ordinary understanding.

Heeding, obeying the Supreme Voice of God sounding within, he conveys to those who come in contact with him the sense of the nearness of God. He inspires them so completely with that immanence that they are impelled to imitate him in accepting the dictates of that divine being. He who becomes assured of the indwelling God, cannot be perverted from living in the light of God, Their light, too, must be seen of men.

Is there, then, any wonder that the kindliness of heart and head and . hand shown by Abbas Effendi creates corresponding kindliness in his adherents? Is there any wonder that his vast love, for humanity obliges man to love man? To those whose inner eyes are opened, the kingdom of God is on earth, for "the Kingdom of Heaven is within" them.

In himself, his everyday bearing, his ways and words, Abbas Effendi furnishes the modern world with a living object-lesson of the transforming energy of The Light of Love. He has said, "All beside love is but words." In his own person he conveys the proof of his own prophecy that the religion of Bahaism is a religion of deeds, vocalising itself not in syllables but in active signs of The Light in the life. The author of the Fourth Gospel wrote, "The life was the light of men."

He bids his followers to recognise the rays of The Light wherever they may appear; in any country; in the professors of any creed. The Light, the unifying influence, should draw men of all classes and conditions together, by dissolving clouds of difference that tend to separation.

He assures his people that the world has received enlightenment through divinely inspired seers who, from time to time, have appeared. Every religion that has arisen in the world owed its rise to these. Thus every religion is of divine origin. Prophets have proclaimed truth, teachers have unfolded the will of the Highest; each prophet, each teacher, of any religious school, has fulfilled the function of a lamp through which The Light has shone upon men.

The history of belief has in it many chapters concerning the rise and progress of religions and has been compelled to add many other chapters bearing upon the fact that the value of each religion, from a spiritual point of view, has lessened and dwindled because of the growth around it of the fungi of superstition and the frequently deadening effect of reverence for ritual. These inevitably shade the shining of The Light and prevent its irradiance. Thus life, created and moved by light, becomes dull in sympathy with the dimness of The Light. Then, at such periods, a new lamp is necessary; a new prophet passes into being, and the world once again rejoices in One who is made manifest by reason of the luminosity of The Light with which He is privileged to move among men.

By virtue of the light borne by himself, he would lead men on the Path of Peace. His light shines full upon the oneness of man with God.

If climatic and geographical considerations have produced antagonism, it is certain that a creed in one quarter has created a crux in another. Men's vision, obscured by films that have imposed themselves upon faith, could not descry hope in one another's outlook. Spiritual perception required, in these latter days, a fresh and lustrous exposition of The Eternal Light. Hence the coming of The Bab, the succession of Baha'u'llah, the culminating influence of Abbas Effendi, who spends himself making clear to men the solidarity of the race as one with each other and with God. His life is his lesson. He lops off no limb of religion from the body of mankind. He urges men to be true to that aspect of the highest that appeals to them; for the core of each creed is truth; the seed of each religion was sown by the Lord.

That Baha'u'llah acted wisely and well in proclaiming his son Abbas Effendi his successor, events have plentifully proved.

Courteous, kindly, dignified, his personality fascinates and compels towards goodness.

Honourable and just, he so disarms prejudice that "his jailers have become his friends." That the people of Acca esteem him and look to him for sympathy and justice might be supposed, but it is a remarkable and noteworthy fact to record that equal esteem is evinced for him by successive governors of the city and by military officers in authority there.

Nearly forty years he has dwelt, imprisoned, in that little city of Acca, a familiar figure, a marked man. Familiarity has not bred contempt, but sincerest admiration and reverence.

Those who have visited him—when the powers that were permitted such visits—have found their love and respect for him increase day by day, even month by month. Prolonged intimacy is the severest of all tests, but, tried by this test, Abbas Effendi is, throughout, the gainer.

Always under surveillance, frequently under suspicion (of political or other inimical intent), his courage has disarmed espionage, and his untiring faculty for forgiving has rendered suspicion foolish.

His devotion and attention to his people have increased rather than lessened during the years of a busy, harassed life. Through persecution, misapprehension, and many misrepresentations, he has proved true to his ideal; unswerving in the pursuance of his purpose.

His liberality relative to varying creeds is equalled by his generosity to friends and foes. Poverty and suffering exist, he considers, in order to be relieved at any personal cost

30

and inconvenience. Those who have vehemently opposed and strenuously fought to hinder him, have participated in much material benefit at his hands. Intolerance is, in the rule of the Bahai, the one impossible word.

In dealing with conflicting opinions and rituals, Abbas Effendi's method is that of acute intelligence and spiritual perception. He exercises his fine insight into the minds of others; an insight as sympathetic as it is immediate. Thus he treats any theme under discussion from the point of view of the religion professed by the enquirer, selecting, as arguments, texts from the Scripture sacred to that religion.

All that is evil or untoward in a man's or a country's condition, he comprehends, deplores, forthwith strives to remedy.

His advanced scientific and hygienic principles have aided him, prisoner and poor, to redeem Acca, at least in part, from its notorious insalubrity.

In signs and miracles he deals not at all. Gifted to no small extent with healing powers—largely the result of education and experience in suffering—he firmly deprecates any imputation of the supernatural.

"If men's minds are fixed on miracles, which prove nothing in themselves, they will be less open to the reception of truth, or be closed entirely to the Divine Message."

How far the sweetness and light of that message as delivered by The Bab, the enlightening revelations of Baha'u'llah, and the Gospel according to Abbas Effendi, have permeated the Persian conscience or penetrated into other Oriental castes, concerns our present purpose but little. The last named of these, however, rejoices with exceeding joy in the promised, and promising, Constitutions of Eastern countries. "For the first time during seven years," writes a devoted friend from Acca in the autumn of 1908, "our Lord has been allowed to visit the tomb of Baha'u'llah. With him I saw the tomb and was permitted to share in his freedom and that of his people."

The chains of the captivity are released. Freedom, to live here or to live there; Freedom, to speak and write tidings of goodwill; Freedom—the word, the thing—cannot be entered into by men who have been born and who have lived, free. It cannot be adequately put into any language. It can only be enjoyed to the uttermost by those to whom liberty has been a lifelong hope, a lifelong sacred dream which the Infinite One in His infinite goodness might make real. It can only become real to those who, like the Bahais, have "suffered and are strong," because of a supreme faith in a supreme cause.

Freedom, liberty, light;—not for one tribe or worshippers in one temple, but for all the sons of men and of God;—these are the one desire of Abdul Baha, Abbas Effendi. His acute. apprehension of man's soul urges him to preach that no people are so distrustful of others as those who, isolated and self-contained, know little, and care less, of contact with other folk. It is their natural tendency to become more and more satisfied with their limitations and indeed to believe at last that material and spiritual salvation can only be acquired within those limits. Upheavals are essential. The advent of a prophet is a necessity; first, perhaps, to be despised, doubted; but, in the end, to cause a vital current of opinion to flow in the direction of charitable speculation. It is true that the parochialist in religion usually uplifts his voice clamorously against the prophet and the prophecy. It is true, too, that when a master-mind frames truth in a new setting, or boldly breaks away incrustations which have longtime concealed truth, and been adored in mistake for truth, a storm of disapproval attempts to drown the missioner's voice and mar his message. Limitations, too frequently the accumulation of custom, convention, or superstition, have, on requisite occasion, to be shattered;

with all courtesy, with all generosity, but with unyielding decision. It is essential to the welfare of the world that seers should arise to utter the truth that has existed from the beginning; the truth that has always, to less extent or more, been uttered in the East.

Out of the East, Abbas Effendi's humanising, spiritualising influence is spreading near and far. In the Eastern firmament a Star has again arisen and its beams are shedding light upon the dark places of the earth.

Each philosophy has many facets. Diamond-wise, the philosophy of Bahaism has been skilfully wrought by experts in prayer and practice.

For example;—Abbas Effendi has been entitled "His Highness the Master"; he prefers to be known as "The Servant," and, day by day, holds himself in readiness to serve. Customary Mohammedan observances are maintained "for the sake of peace and to avoid the imputation of social innovation." Constant generosity is enjoined. These are facets of jewels shining in the Bahai crown.

Monogamy is advised, and Abbas Effendi's example is respected and admired.

Differences of religious opinion should be disregarded; most of all when charity (alms-giving) is concerned.

Each Bahai should have good working knowledge of some useful trade or profession. Industry is expected of all. The emancipation of woman and the equal education of girls and boys is Abbas Effendi's desire and prophecy. Cleanliness of body and mind; practical thrift; personal action towards universal Brotherhood;—these are parts of the clauses in the holy ordinance.

# THE SEVEN VALLEYS

THE written word of Baha'u'llah is possessed of much direct instruction, conveyed very beautifully, having always a helpful and inspiring note.

Let us wander, if you will, for a little time, with him in "The Seven Valleys," seven stations, so to speak, on the Divine Way. We shall find these stations in a veritable Garden of the Soul. They are described in the form of answers to questions put by a mystic Sufi, a Mohammedan named Sheik Abdur Rahman. Our gleanings from these answers, or tablets, will be gathered from Ali Kuli Khan's translation, issued by the Bahai Publishing Society in 1906. We will note that these answers are further described as "revealed"; that, naturally they are presented with a glowing and ornate Oriental wealth of imagery. Much of this we must leave ungarnered, contenting ourselves with enough of the real fineness of the work to give us a clear conception of the thought behind it.

It begins thus "*In the Name of God, the Compassionate, the Merciful.*

Praise be unto God, who caused existence to appear from non-existence, inscribed the mysteries of the existence on the tablet of Man and taught him the explanation of that which he knoweth not. . . . I mention unto thee holy, brilliant allusions from the Stations of Glory; so that they may attract thee unto the court of holiness, nearness, and beauty, and draw thee unto a state wherein thou shalt see naught in existence but the countenance of His Highness thy Beloved One. . . . That is the station of which the

34

nightingale of unity hath sung, viz., 'And there shall appear upon the tablet of thine heart the traces of the subtle mysteries of 'fear God and God will instruct you.' . . . May it do good unto me, unto thee, unto whomsoever may ascend to the heaven of knowledge, and to him whose heart is fascinated by the zephyr of assurance wafting upon the garden of his innate heart, from the Sheba of the Merciful.

*Peace be unto those who follow guidance."*

It must be remarked that "the stages of the journey of travellers from the earthly dwelling to the Divine House have been designated to be Seven; some have spoken of these as 'Seven Valleys' . . . and they have said, 'Not until the traveller migrates from self and accomplishes these journeys, will he arrive at the sea of nearness and union.'

### *The First Valley:*

### THE VALLEY OF SEARCH

The steed upon which to journey through this valley is Patience.

In this journey the traveller will reach no destination without patience, nor will he attain to his aim. He must never be dejected.

Were he to endeavour for a hundred thousand years, and see not the beauty of the Friend, he must not be downhearted.

It is conditional upon these servants to purify their hearts which are the source of the Divine Treasury from every blemish, to turn away from blind imitation which is a trace of forefathers and ancestors; and to close the doors of friendship and enmity with all the peoples of the earth.

In this journey the seeker reaches such a station that he finds all the existing beings bewildered in search of the Friend.

Many a Jacob he sees wandering in quest of Joseph. A world of friends he beholds, who are running in search of the Desired One, and a universe of lovers he finds, who are journeying after the Beloved One.

At every moment he perceives a new matter, and at every hour he becomes informed of a mystery; for he has lifted his heart from both worlds and intended to attain the Ka'aba (the goal) of the Beloved.

At every step the assistance of the Invisible surrounds him, and the ardour of his search increases."

As illustrating the thoroughness of seeking requisite for attainment in the First Valley, a story is given, prefaced by the statement:

"Search should be measured by the deed of the Majnoon of love."

"Majnoon," our translator tells us, signifies "insane," and was the name by which a celebrated lover belonging to the old Arabian nomadic tribes was known. His object was Laila, the daughter of an Arab prince. The story is "symbolical of pure, human love in its highest degree, and has been the theme of many Persian poets. Nizami's poem on this love story is the masterpiece."

"It is related that one day Majnoon was seen sifting the dust and shedding tears. They said, 'What art thou doing?' He said, 'I am searching for Laila!' They said, 'Woe unto thee! Laila is from the pure spirit, and thou art seeking her in the earth!' He said, 'I exert myself in her search *everywhere*; perchance I may find her somewhere!'"

"Although seeking the Lord of Lords in the dust is contemptible to the wise, yet it is evidence of utmost endeavour and search. 'Whoso seeks with diligence shall surely find.'

A sincere seeker finds naught save union with the Desired One, and a lover has no aim but to attain to the beloved.

A seeker cannot obtain this (spirit of) search, except by the sacrifice of all that exists; that is, he must annihilate all that he has seen, heard, or understood, with "the negation 'no,' so that he may reach the city of the Spirit, which is the city of 'but.'"

Here our translator reminds us that "There is no God but God" is the formula of faith in the Divine Unity. "There is *no* God" is denial and negation, while "*but* God" is faith and affirmation.

"An effort is needed that we may exert ourselves in search for Him, and an endeavour that we may taste of the honey of union with Him. If we drink of this cup we shall forget the whole world.

In this journey the traveller sits on every soil and dwells in every land, and seeks the beauty of the Friend in every face.

He searches for the Beloved One in every country; he joins every multitude . . . perchance he may discover the mystery of the Beloved One in some head, or behold the beauty of the Desired One in some visage.

If, through the assistance of God, he find, in this journey, a trace of the Traceless Friend . . . he will immediately step into the Valley of Love and become melted with the fire of love.

37

## The Second Valley:

### THE VALLEY OF LOVE

In this valley the heaven of attraction is lifted up, the world-illuminating sun of longing dawns forth and the fire of love becomes ablaze.

And when the fire of love is become ablaze, the harvest of reason will be wholly consumed.

At this time the traveller is unconscious, both of himself and of aught else save himself.

He knows neither knowledge nor ignorance, neither doubt nor certainty; neither does he recognise the morn of guidance nor the eve of error.

He avoids both infidelity and faith.

Thus it is said by Attar (one of the great, inspired Sufi leaders, poets and philosophers of the middle ages of Islam), 'Leave infidelity to the infidel and faith to the faithful; a single particle of pain, in thy love, is enough for the heart of Attar.'

The steed of this valley is Pain.

Without pain this journey will never be accomplished.

In this stage the lover has no thought but of the Beloved One, and seeks no shelter but the Desired One. At every moment he freely gives a hundred lives in the path of the Beloved, and at every step he throws a thousand at the feet of the Friend.

'O my brother! not until thou enterest the Egypt of the Spirit wilt thou attain, to the Joseph of the beauty of the Friend; not until thou, like Jacob, give up thine outward

38

eye, wilt thou open thine inward eye; and not until thou art ablaze with the fire of love wilt thou associate with the Friend of Ecstasy.

A lover fears nothing, and no loss can do him harm.

Thou wilt see him cool in fire, and find him dry even in the sea.

Love accepts not any existence, nor wishes any life; he finds life in death, and glory in shame.

Much wit is needed to make one worthy of the ardour of love; and many a head is required to be fit for the noose of the Friend. Blessed is the neck which falleth into His noose, and happy is the head which is dropped on the dust in the path of His love.

Be alien to thyself, that thou mayest find thy way to the Incomparable One.

Abandon the mortal earth, that thou mayest take residence in the Divine Nest.

*Nothingness* is needed until thou mayest kindle the fire of existence and become acceptable in the path of love. 'Love does not accept a soul alive (to material things); a falcon preys not on a dead mouse.'

At every moment Love consumes a world; and in whatever land he hoists his banner, he makes it desolate.

Existence has no being in his realm, and men of reason have no foothold in his dominion.

The whale of love swallows up the erudite in reason, and destroys the prudent in knowledge. It quaffs the 'Seven Seas'; and yet the thirst of its heart is not allayed and still it says, 'Is there yet any more?'

It becomes alien to self; and shuns all that is in the world.
. . .

Therefore the veils of the Satanic ego must needs be consumed with the fire of love; so that the spirit may become clean and purified for comprehending the grades of the Lord of 'but for thee.'" [Here the reader must be referred to the translator's note: "But for thee"—a tradition, relating the words of God to the Prophet (Mohammed), "*But for thee*, I would not have created the spheres!" (traditional).] "Kindle thou a fire of love and consume all possessions (or Self); then lift thy foot and step into the mountain of the lovers." [Here our translator informs us that Baha'u'llah is quoting from one of his own odes.]

"If, by the assistance of the Creator, the lover is released in safety from the claws of the falcon of Love, he will then arrive at the realm of the Valley of Divine Knowledge.


### *The Third Valley:*

#### THE VALLEY OF DIVINE KNOWLEDGE

He will be led from doubt to certainty, and directed from the darkness of the error of worldly desire to the light of guidance of piety.

His inner eye will be opened, and he will engage in close communion with his Beloved.

He will open the portal of truth and devotion and close the doors of superficiality.

In this state he will yield to the Divine Decree, will see war as peace, find the Significances of life in death, perceive the mysteries of the "other world" in the regions of creation

40

. . . with the outward and inward eye; and, with a spiritual heart he will behold the Eternal Wisdom in the infinite manifestations of God.

In an ocean he will see a drop, and in a drop he will detect the mysteries of an ocean.

'The core of whatever mote thou mayest split, therein thou wilt find a sun.'

In this valley, through absolute vision, a traveller does not see in God's creation any difference or contradiction; and at every moment he will say, 'Thou canst not see, in the creation of the Most Merciful One, any difference. Turn thou thine eyes whether thou can see any flaws!' (Koran).

He will see justice in injustice and witness grace in justice; he will find many a knowledge concealed in ignorance. . . .

He will break the cage of body and desire, and be attached to the spirit of the people of immortality. He will ascend on ideal ladders, and hasten to the heaven of Significances. .

If he experience any oppression he will endure it with patience, and if he see any wrath he will show forth affection. . . .

The people of the valley beyond this see the beginning and the end as one; nay, rather, they see no beginning and no end; 'without beginning without end. . . .'

As it is said, 'A perfect realisation of Divine Unity is to strip it from all attributes. . . .'

Hence, in this connection, Khaji Abd-'Allah has set forth a subtle point and consummation in his interpretation of the verse 'Direct us in the Right Way' (Koran), and it is this: 'Point unto us the right way, that is bless us with Love, thine Essence; so that, becoming free from all regard for ourselves, and for all else save Thee, we may be wholly captivated by Thee, so as to know none but Thee, to see naught save Thee, to think of naught beside Thee.' (Khaji Abd-'Allah was, adds Ali Kuli Khan, a high, mystic Sufi leader, of the house of Ansar, in the middle ages of Islam. His tomb is situated in Herat. 'Ansar' literally means 'helpers';—hence, a term denominating those people of Medina who first believed in Mohammed.)

Nay, they pass even beyond this station, as it is said, 'Love is a screen between the lover and the Beloved.' . . .

At this time the morn of knowledge hath dawned, and the lamps of travelling and wayfaring are put out."

At this point we are bidden to note that "travelling and wayfaring after truth, under the direction of the Sufi leaders, are of the characteristics of mystic Sufis. These leaders, Sufis call 'lights,' whereby to find the truth. But the appearance of the manifestations of God is that of the Sun of Truth itself. Hence it is said by Ali, 'Quench the light (lamp) when the Sun hath already dawned.' Here Baha'u'llah teaches that in these days men must depend on the Sun of Truth which has become manifest.

If thou art a man of prayer and supplication, fly on the wings of saintly effort, so that thou mayest see the mysteries of the Friend, and attain to the light of the Beloved.

'We are God's, and unto Him shall we surely return.'

After journeying through the Valley of Knowledge, which is the last station of limitation, the traveller reaches the first stage of the Valley of Divine Unity.

## The Fourth Valley:

### THE VALLEY OF DIVINE UNITY

He (the traveller) drinks from the cup of abstraction and gazes on the manifestations of singleness.

At this station he rends asunder the veils of plurality, flies away from the worlds of lust, and ascends to the Heaven of Oneness:

He hears with Divine ears, and beholds the mysteries of the creation of the Eternal One with God-like eyes. He steps into the retreat of the Friend, and becomes an intimate in the pavilion of the Beloved. . . .

He sees no commendation, name, or dignity, of himself; he sees his own commendation in the commendation of the True One, and beholds the Name of the True One in his own name. He will know 'all voices to be from the King,' and hear all the melodies from Him.

He will be established on the throne of—'Say, all is from God,' and rest on the carpet of—'There is no power nor might but through God alone.'

He will look upon things with the vision of oneness . . . and see the light of unity manifest and present in all the existent things. All the differences which the traveller sees in the world of Being during the various stages of his journey, are due to the view of the traveller himself. We bring an illustration in order that this fact may become thoroughly evident:

Consider the phenomenal sun which shines forth on all beings with the same effulgence. . . .

But its appearance in every place and the light it sheds thereon, is in accord with the degree of the capacity of that place. In a mirror it reflects . . . it creates fire in the crystal

. . . it develops everything according to the capacity of that thing; by the command of the Causer of effects.

Colours also appear in accord with (the nature of) the place; even as in a yellow glass the splendour is yellow, in a white one the ray is white, and in a red one it is red. These differences are due to the place and not to the effulgence of light; and if the place is confronted by an obstacle, such as walls or ceiling, that place is bereft of the splendour of the sun.

Some weak souls, having enclosed the ground of knowledge within the wall of self and desire, and within the veil of heedlessness and blindness, are therefore screened from the effulgence of the Sun of Significances and the mysteries of the Eternal Beloved One; are kept from the Gems of wisdom . . . deprived of Beauty, and separated from the Ka'aba (sanctum) of Glory. . . .

An agreeable odour is unpleasant to the beetle, and a fragrant perfume has no effect upon one afflicted with a cold.

Hence, for the guidance of the multitude, it has been said, 'Remove the cold from thy head and brain, so that the Fragrance of God may fill thy nostrils.'

The difference of place is now made clear.

When the gaze of the traveller is restricted, when he looks through glasses (of different colours) he sees yellow, red, or white.

It is due to such a view of things that conflict is stirred up . . . and a gloomy dust, rising from men of limitations, has enveloped the world.

Some extend their gaze to the effulgence of the light; and others drink from the wine of Oneness and therefore see nothing but the sun itself.

Because of journeying in these different stations, travellers differ in their understanding and explanation of things.

That is why the sign of difference is manifest in the world; for some dwell on the plane of oneness and speak of the world of oneness; some stand in the worlds of limitation, others in the stages of self, and still others are absolutely veiled.

The ignorant, who have gained no portion from the splendour of the Beautiful One, speak in certain (unreasonable) words, and in every time and age they inflict upon the people of Unity that which is only worthy of and befits their own selves.

'If God should punish men for their iniquity, He would not leave (on the earth) any moving thing; but He giveth them respite unto an appointed time' (Koran).

A pure heart is like unto a mirror; purify it with the polish of Love, and severance from all save God, until the Ideal Sun may reflect therein, and the Eternal Morn may dawn.

Then wilt thou find clear and manifest the meaning of— 'Neither doth My earth nor heaven occupy Me, but the heart of My faithful servant occupieth Me!'—and wilt take thy life in thy hands and sacrifice it, with a thousand longings, to the new Beloved.

When the lights of the splendour of the King of Oneness are seated on the throne of the heart and soul, His light becomes manifest in all the parts and members.

Then will the mystery of the (following) tradition emerge from the veil of obscurity:

'A servant always draws near Me with prayers, until I respond unto him. And when I have responded to him, then I become his ear wherewith he heareth.'

For (in this case) the Owner of the house becomes manifest in His Own House (*i.e.* the heart), and the pillars of the house are all illuminative and radiative through His light.

The action and effect of the Light is from the Giver of Light; this is why all move through Him, and arise by His Desire.

This is that Fountain wherefrom drink those near unto God; as it is said, 'A Fountain whereof those shall drink who are near (unto God).'

Let no one suppose these explanations to be redolent of anthropomorphism, or indicative of a degrading or restricting of the worlds (or states) of the True One to the planes of the creatures . . . for God, in His Essence, is sanctified above ascent or descent, entrance or exit. He has been, and will be everlastingly independent of (or free from) the attributes of the creatures.

No one has known Him, and no soul has found out His substance.

All the sages are bewildered in the Valley of His Knowledge, and all the saints are perplexed (in their endeavours to) comprehend His Essence. He is purified from being comprehended by all men of comprehension, and is exalted above the knowing of men of knowledge.

'The road (to His Essence) is barred, and search (therefor) is rejected.

His evidence is His Sign, and His Being is His proof.'

Thus the lovers of the Face of the Beloved One have said, 'O Thou whose essence alone bears evidence of the Essence of Him who is sanctified beyond homogeneity with His creatures.' . . .

How can a mortal shadow compare with the Immortal Sun?

Yea, such mentions as are made concerning the stages of knowledge, concern only the knowledge of the splendour of that Sun of Truth which becomes manifest in the mirrors (*i.e.* prophets, manifestations).

The reflection of that Light is within the hearts; but it is veiled through sensual coverings and accidental conditions; as is the case with a light enclosed within an iron lantern. When the lantern is removed the radiance of the light will appear.

Likewise, when one rends asunder the illusive veils from the face of the heart, the light of oneness will dwell therein.

Wherefore it is known that even for the Splendour (of the Sun of Divine Essence) there is no entrance nor exit; how much less for that Essence of Beings and that Mystery of the Desired One.

Reflect upon these stations with verification, and not with blind imitation.

The repellent 'avaunt' of words cannot repulse the traveller (after Truth), nor can the terror of allusions impede him.

'What veil can stand between the lover and the Beloved? The Wall of Alexander itself can be no obstacle or screen.'

Mysteries are many, and strangers are countless.

Books are not sufficient for the Mystery of the Beloved, nor can it be exhausted in these Tablets, although it is no more than one word, and but one allegory.

'Knowledge is but one point, but the ignorant have multiplied it.'

I do not wish to mention much of the former sayings; for to speak of the sayings of others would be an evidence of acquired learning (*i.e.* mediate knowledge), and not of the Divine Gift (*i.e.* immediate knowledge).

Moreover such explanations are beyond the limits of this treatise.

My forbearing to speak of the sayings of others is not due to pride, but because of a showing forth of Wisdom and a manifesting of the Gift. . . .

This servant accounts himself as nothing, even in the court of one of the beloved of God (*i.e.* believers); how much more so in the presence of the 'Holy Ones'?

Praise be unto my Lord, the Supreme. . . .

Although a short illustration has already been given as to the beginning and end of the relative or dependent (not absolute) world (or plane), yet again we set another example, so that all of the meanings may become manifest in the garment of illustration.

For instance . . . consider . . . how you are the first in relation to your son, and the last in relation to your father; how, outwardly (*i.e.* according to the soul), (you bear evidence) of the inward mysteries which, as a Divine Gift, are deposited within you.

Consequently, being the first, the last, the manifest, the hidden, becomes true of you in the sense set forth above; so that in these four grades bestowed on you, you may comprehend the (corresponding) grades of the Divine; . . . 'Verily! He is the First and the Last, the Manifest and the Hidden!'

The First is identical with the Last, and the Last is the same as the First.

'Enkindle a fire with the Love of the Beloved One, and consume therewith every thought and pious work.'

Consider thine own self; if thou hadst not become a father nor seen a son, thou wouldest not have heard even these words.

Now, therefore, forget all these, so that thou mayest learn in the School of Unity, before the Instructor of Love, and come back from the stage—'Verily, we are (from God)'— unto ('and to Him) we return.'

Thus thou mayest abandon the abode of Unreality, and attain into thine own real station, and abide in the shade of the Tree of Knowledge.

Impoverish thyself so that thou mayest arrive at the Court of Affluence.

Humiliate the body, so that thou mayest drink from the River of Glory, and attain unto all the meanings of the poems which thou hast questioned.

It is evident that these states depend upon the view of the traveller.

In every city he sees a world; in every valley he comes upon a fountain; in every desert he hears a melody.

Peace be on whomsoever accomplisheth this supreme journey, and followeth the True One through the Lights of Guidance.


### *The Fifth Valley:*

## THE VALLEY OF CONTENTMENT

In this valley he (the traveller) discovers the breezes of

Divine Contentment, which waft from the desert of the Spirit, and consume the veils of poverty.

There he witnesses the day wherein 'God will make all independent out of His abundance.'

(He will witness this day) with his outward and inward eye in the visible and invisible parts of things. He passes from sadness to joy; and he changes depression and dejection into gladness and cheerfulness.

Though the travellers in this valley outwardly dwell on the earth, yet inwardly they recline on the high couch of Significances, and they partake of ideal, imperishable benefits, and quaff pure, spiritual wines.

The tongue is unable to give an account of these three (last) valleys, and utterance falls exceeding short. The pen cannot step into this court, and the ink gives no result but blackness.

Concerning these states the nightingale of the heart has other melodies and mysteries which set the heart in agitation and the spirit in uproar.

But this enigma of Significances must be only revealed from heart to heart, and confided from breast to breast.

Heart alone can communicate to heart the state of the knower (of divine secrets); this is not the work of a messenger, nor can this be contained in letters. On many points I keep silent because of my inability; to state them is beyond speech, and if I say them my words would be insufficient.

Not until thou reachest the garden of these Significances wilt thou taste of the immortal wine of this valley. If thou tastest thereof thou wilt close thine eyes to all strangers, and drink from the wine of contentment. Thou wilt sever thyself from all, and become united with Him; give up thy life in His Way, and pour out thy soul freely;—although there is no stranger in this station, that thou shouldest close thine eyes; 'There was but God, but there was nothing with Him.' Because, in this stage, the traveller beholds the beauty of the Friend in everything.

In fire he sees the Face of the Beloved; in unreality perceives the sign of the Reality; and through the attributes he witnesses the Mystery of the Divine Substance (or Essence), for he has consumed the veils with a mere sigh, and removed the coverings with a single gaze.

He looks upon the new creation with a discerning sight; and comprehends subtle signs with a pure heart.

'At that Day we will make thy sight discerning,'—is an evidence of this saying, and is sufficient for this instance."

[The Valley of Contentment is sometimes translated as the Valley of Richness.]

"After traversing the Valley of Pure Contentment, the traveller reaches the Valley of Astonishment.

### The Sixth Valley:

#### THE VALLEY OF ASTONISHMENT

He plunges in the sea of grandeur and at every moment his amazement increases.

Now he sees the body of affluence as indigence itself, and the essence of independence as impotence. Now he becomes astonished at the beauty of the All-glorious, and now he loathes his own being.

Many are the trees of Significances uprooted by the blast of astonishment, and many are the souls it exhausted.

For this valley sets the traveller in agitation.

But such appearances are highly beloved and esteemed in the eye of one who has attained.

At every moment he witnesses a wonderful world and a New Creation, he adds astonishment upon astonishment and he becomes dazed at the new creation of the King of Oneness.

If we reflect upon any of the creations we shall behold a hundred thousand consummate wisdoms, and learn a hundred thousand knowledges.

One of these is that of Sleep (or dreams): consider what mysteries are deposited therein, what wisdoms are stored therein.

Consider. You sleep in a certain house, the doors of which are closed.

Suddenly you find yourself in a remote city; you enter it without motion of the feet or exhaustion of the body; you see without troubling the eyes; you hear without distressing the ears; and you speak without the use of the tongue.

There are times when it happens that—ten years thereafter—you will witness outwardly in the world what thou hast seen at this night in a dream.

Now there are many wisdoms visible in this dream; but others than the people of this valley cannot comprehend them as they are.

First; what is that world, wherein, without eye, ear, hand or tongue, one realises the purpose of these senses?

Secondly; this day thou seest in the world of reality the effect of a dream which thou hast experienced years ago in the world of dreams.

Reflect upon the differences of these two worlds, and the mysteries deposited therein; so that thou mayest attain unto the confirmations and revelations of the Glorified One, and enter into the World of Holiness.

God, the Exalted, has placed these signs within the creatures, so that philosophers may not deny the mysteries of the After Life, and not make light of that whereunto they have been promised.

For some have clung to reason, and deny whatever cannot be grasped by reason; although the feeble reason can never comprehend these same aforesaid conditions, but only the Universal, Supreme Reason (can do so).

'How can finite reason comprehend the Koran? How can a spider hunt a Simurgh?'"

[A "Simurgh"—a griffin; a fabulous bird; the conception of the largest and rarest of birds; mythologically conceived as inhabiting the lofty peaks of Mount Caucasus.]

"All these worlds (*i.e.* conditions) will present themselves in the Valley of Astonishment, and, at every moment, the traveller seeks for an increase of such, without becoming exhausted.

Hence the 'Lord of those gone by and those who are to come' has said concerning the grades of reflection and the declaration of astonishment—'O Lord! Increase my astonishment in Thee!'

Likewise; ponder over the completeness of the creation of man; all these worlds and all these grades are enveloped and concealed in him.

'Dost thou think thy body a small thing, while in thee is enfolded the universe?'

Then an effort is needed that we annihilate the animal condition, in order that the meaning of the human may become manifest.

Likewise Lokman, who drank from the fount of Wisdom and tasted of the sea of Mercy, in demonstrating the states of resurrection to his son Nathan, gave the dream (or sleep) as a proof, and applied it as an illustration.

We speak of it in this place, so that this humble servant may leave here a mention of that youth of the school of Unity, who was aged in the stages of instruction and abstraction.

He said: 'O Son! if thou be not able to sleep, thou wilt not be able to die; and if thou canst manage to not awake from sleep, thou canst manage to not resurrect after death.'

The heart is a store of divine mysteries.

Make it not a receptacle for mortal thoughts, and consume not the capital of the precious life by occupying yourself with this evanescent world. Thou art of the World of Holiness; attach not thy heart unto the earth.

Thou art a denizen of the Court of Nearness; choose not an earthly home.

In fine, there is no end to mentioning these grades, and this servant has no composure on account of the injuries done by the people of the world.

'This speech remained unfinished and incomplete. I am disheartened and downcast—O forbear!'

The pen laments and the ink weeps, and the river of the heart rolls with waves of blood.

Naught shall befall us, save that which God hath decreed unto us!

Peace be upon those who follow Guidance.

(The Valley of Astonishment is sometimes translated as The Valley of Perplexity.)

After ascending to the lofty heights of Astonishment the traveller arrives at the Valley of Absolute Poverty and Annihilation.


### The Seventh Valley:

#### THE VALLEY OF ABSOLUTE POVERTY AND ANNIHILATION

This is the station of dying from self, and living through God; of being poor of one's self, and rich in the Desired One.

In this station poverty is mentioned as meaning one's indigence in all that is of the world of creation; and one's affluence in all that is of the worlds of Truth.

For when a sincere lover and agreeable friend attains to the meeting of the beloved and desired one, a fire is enkindled from the radiance of the beauty of the beloved and the heat of the heart of the lover, which consumes all coverings and veils.

Nay, whatever is with him, even marrow and skin, will thereby be burnt, and naught remain except the friend.

'When the attributes of the Ancient One became manifest,

then the Interlocutor (Moses) consumed the attributes of all things accidental.'

In this station the one who has attained is sanctified from all that pertaineth to the world.

If, therefore, those who have attained to the Sea of Union do not possess any of the limited things of this mortal world: be these things of material belongings or of selfish thoughts: there is no harm in that.

For whatever is possessed by men is confined within its own limits; whereas that which is God's is sanctified (from all limitations).

Much reflection should be bestowed on this explanation in order that the end may become manifest. . . .

This station is that of Poverty, of which it is said, 'Poverty is my glory' (Mohammed).

Many are the meanings and grades of the outward and inward poverty, which I do not deem appropriate to be mentioned in this place, and which I therefore reserve for some other time; if God will, and the Divine Decree may ordain.

It is in this stage that the traces of all things are destroyed in the traveller, and the Beauty of the Face unveils itself from the Orient of the Eternal World, and the meaning of 'Everything is mortal save the Face of God' becomes manifest.

Hearken to the melodies of the Spirit with all thy heart and soul, and preserve them as the sight of thine eyes; for the Divine Enlightenments will not always flow, like the vernal rain, upon the soil of human hearts.

Although the bounty of the Bountiful One is continual and free from interruption; yet for every time and age a certain portion is determined and a certain benefit is ordained; and these are bestowed (on men) according to a certain quantity and measure.

'There is no thing but the storehouses thereof are in Our Hands, and we distribute not the same save in a determinate measure' (Koran).

The cloud of the Mercy of the Beloved One will pour down only on the Garden of the Soul, and it will not bestow this bounty except in times of Spring.

Other seasons have no portion of this mightiest Grace, and barren soils have no share in this Favour.

Not every sea has pearls; not every branch brings forth flowers; nor doth the nightingale sing thereon.

Therefore, so long as the nightingale of the spiritual planting hath not returned to the Divine Rose-Garden, and the Lights of the Spiritual Dawn have not returned to the Sun of Reality;—make an effort.

Perchance in this mortal land thou mayest inhale a fragrance from the Immortal Rose-Garden, and rest for ever under the shade of the people of this valley (city).

When thou hast reached this lofty, exalted grade and attained to this great station, then wilt thou see the Friend, and forget strangers (*i.e.* all else save Him).

'The Friend, unveiled, is manifest from every door and wall (everywhere), O ye possessors of Sight!'

Then thou hast abandoned the drop of life and reached the ocean of the Beloved One.

This is the goal which thou hast demanded; God willing, thou mayest attain thereunto.

In this Valley even the veils of Light are rent asunder and vanish.

'To His Beauty there are no veils but Light, and His Face has no covering save manifestation.'

How wonderful that the Well-Beloved is manifest as the sun, while strangers are in search of vanities and riches.

Yea! He is concealed by the intensity of manifestation, and He is hidden by the ardour of Emanation.

'The True One hath become manifest, like unto the shining sun. Pity that He hath come in the city of the blind!'

In this valley the traveller journeys through the stages of 'Oneness of Existence' and of Appearance, and will attain to a Oneness which is sanctified above both these stations." ["The mystic doctrine of the 'Oneness of Existence' is outlined from this formula—'*Only God exists; He is in all things, and all things are in Him.*'"—NOTE by TRANSLATOR.]

"(The condition of) Ecstasy can penetrate this saying, but not controversy nor conflict.

He who hath chosen an abode in this Meeting, or discovered a breeze from this Garden, knoweth what I say.

In all these journeys the traveller must not deviate . . . but must cling to the hem of obedience to the (Divine) Commandments, and lay firm hold of the rope of shunning things forbidden by the Law. . . .

Although these journeys have no visible termination in the world of time, yet, if the Invisible Assistance vouchsafe a devoted traveller (lit. one severed from all else save God), and if the Guardian of the Command (*i.e.* the manifestation of God) help him, he will traverse these seven stages in only seven steps; nay, in seven breaths; nay, even in one breath (a moment) if God will or desire. 'This is through His Bounty to whomsoever He willeth.'

Those who soar in the sky of Oneness, and who have attained to the Sea of Abstraction, have accounted this station, which is the station in this city of Immortality in God, to be the ultimate destination of the Arif—(one who is intimate with highest mystic thought)—and the ultimate home of the Lovers.

But, to this humble (nit of the Sea of Significances, this station is only the first city-wall of the heart; that is, the first arrival of man at the City of the Heart.

Four stages have been assigned to the heart, of which we will make mention. There will be found those who are intimate with such mysteries.

'When the pen reached the point of describing this state, the pen broke and the paper was torn.'

This gazelle of the desert of Oneness is chased by many hounds, and this nightingale of the Garden of Eternity is followed by many beaks; the crow of oppression is lain in ambush for this bird of the Sky of Divinity, and this prey of the Wilderness of Love is pursued by the hunter of jealousy.

Make an effort; perchance it may, as a globe, protect this lamp from contrary winds; although it is the hope of this lamp to shine in the Divine Glass and to be ablaze in the Ideal Niche.

For a neck which is lifted in the Love of God, will certainly be severed by a sword; a head which is raised in Love will assuredly blown by the winds; and the heart which is linked to the commemoration of the Beloved will certainly be full of grief.

How well it is said (by the poet):

'Live on free (from love), for the very repose of love is distress;
 Its beginning is pain, and its end is death.'

*Peace be upon those who follow Guidance.*

If thou hearest the melodies of this mortal bird, thou wilt seek after the Immortal Ever- lasting Chalice, and abandon the mortal and transient cups.

*Peace be upon those who follow Guidance.*

Here is the End of the 'Seven Valleys.'"

Before we leave them for this present time, we will transcribe a note which runs:

"The three stages of Sufi life are as follows:

I. Shariat, *i.e.* Religious Laws; or religious life.

II. Tari-Kat, *i.e.* Travelling in Search of Truth; by finding the Perfect Man who embodies it, and guides men to it. This stage also includes 'hermit' life.

III. Hakirat, *i.e.* Truth; to attain to which, according to Sufis, depends upon passing through the two preceding stages.

Here Baha'u'llah teaches that, contrary to what some Sufis teach or believe, the laws of religion must be the guide even when man has attained the Truth; for Truth itself is embodied in the laws of religion. To abandon the laws in any stage of development would be sheer antinomianism and therefore a great error."

(This note refers to the text above, concerning the error of deviation from commandment.)

Here, too (since they are added to the script of "The Seven Valleys"), we may appropriately place these sayings:

"Empty thyself from that which is caused by thy desire (or lust); then advance towards thy Master.

Purify thyself from all else save Him, so that thou mayest sacrifice thy soul in His Love.

Abstain from the Presence of the True One, if the attributes of the world still remain in thee.

Thank thy Lord on His earth, so that He may thank (bless) thee in His Heaven; although, in the world of Oneness, Heaven is identical with His earth.

Renounce from thyself the limited veils, so that thou mayest know that which thou hast not known of the Stations of Sanctity."

*Peace be upon those who follow Guidance.*

# TEXTS FROM THE TABLETS OF BAHA'U'LLAH

"ASSOCIATION (intercourse) is always conducive to union and harmony; and union and harmony are the cause of the order of the world and the life of nations.

Forbearance and Benevolence . . . are as two lights for the darkness of the world; and as two teachers to lead nations to knowledge.

Good character is, verily, the best mantle for men on the part of God.

Gaze towards Justice and Equity under all circumstances.

Trustworthiness . . . is the door of tranquillity to all the world; the best garment for your temples and the most splendid crown for your heads.

Make not light of any matter, but speak in Truthfulness and Sincerity.

Refuse not to discharge the due reward of any one; respect possessors of talent; stain not tongues with slander.

Knowledge is one of the greatest benefits of God. To acquire knowledge is incumbent on all.

*Tablet of Tarazet*

O people of God! Be not occupied with yourselves. Be

intent on the betterment of the world and the training of nations.

Glory is not his who loves his native land; but glory is his who loves his kind.

Courtesy is the lord of all the virtues.

The deniers and contradictors hold to four words:

First: Destroying men's lives.

Second: Burning the Books.

Third: Shunning other nations.

Fourth: Exterminating other communities.

Now, by the Grace and Authority of the Word of God, these four great barriers have been demolished . . . and God hath changed brutal manners into spiritual qualities.

Certain laws and principles are necessary and indispensable for Persia; but it is suitable that these should be accomplished in accord with the wish of the Shah, the eminent doctors, and the great State authorities.

The fear of God is the real guardian and the ideal protector. Flee from that which is redolent of corruption (or sedition).

*Tablet of the World*

Those souls (mystic Sufis) have affirmed, concerning the stages of Divine Unity, that which is the greatest cause of idleness and superstition. They have, indeed, removed the distinction and have imagined themselves to be God. The True One is sanctified above all; (but) His Signs are manifest in all things. The Signs are *from* Him—not He Himself.

Consider the rays of the sun; its lights have encompassed the world, but these splendours are *from it*, and from its manifestations; they are through itself, but are not itself.

Schools must first train the children in the principles of Religion, so that the Promise and the Threat recorded in the Books of God may prevent them from the things forbidden and adorn them with the mantle of the Commandments; but this in such a measure that it may not injure the children by resulting in ignorant fanaticism and bigotry.

The trustees (members) of the House of Justice must consult upon the ordinances as they are outwardly revealed in the Book, and then enforce of these whatever prove agreeable to them.

Moderation is desirable in every affair.

Consider the civilisation of the people of the Occident— how it has occasioned commotion and agitation. . . . There has appeared an infernal instrument, and atrocity is displayed in the destruction of life. It is impossible to reform these violent evils, except the peoples of the world become united in affairs, or in one Religion.

Praise be to God. A wonderful thing is perceived; the lightning (electricity) and similar forces are subdued by a conductor and act by his command. Exalted is the Mighty One who hath made manifest that which He desired, through His absolute Invincible Command.

Each one of the revealed Commands is a strong fortress for the (protection of the) world.

A solitary life and severe discipline do not meet God's approval. The possessors of perception and knowledge should look to the means which are conducive to joy and fragrance.

Deprive not yourselves of that which is created for you.

Charity is beloved and acceptable before God, and is accounted the chief among all good deeds.

The Reflective Faculty (or the Mind) is the depository of crafts, arts and sciences. Exert yourselves, so that the gems of knowledge and wisdom may proceed from this ideal mine, and conduce to the tranquillity and union of the different nations of the world.

Under all circumstances, whether in adversity or comfort, in glory or affliction . . . show forth love and affection, compassion and union.

*Words of Paradise*

All the former and later Books of God are adorned with His commemoration and speak His praise. Through Him the standard of knowledge is planted in the world, and the Banner of Unity is hoisted among nations.

Knowledge is like unto wings for the being (of man) and is as a ladder for ascending. . . . The possessors of sciences and arts have a great right among the people of the world. Whereunto testifies the Mother of Divine Utterance in the Day of Return. Joy unto those that hear.

Knowledge is the means of honour, prosperity, joy, gladness, happiness and exultation.

He (The Bab) says in description of 'He-whom-God-shall-manifest';—'Verily, He is the One who shall utter in all grades, "Verily, I am God. There is no God but Me, the Lord of all things, and all besides Me is created by Me! O ye My creatures! Ye are to worship Me!"' Likewise, in another place, speaking of 'He-whom-God-shall-manifest,' he says, 'Verily, I (The Bab) am the first one of those who worship Him.'

Now, man must reflect upon the 'Worshipper' (The Bab); and the 'Worshipped One' (Baha'u'llah); perchance the people of the earth may attain to a drop of the Sea of Knowledge, and comprehend the Station of this Manifestation. Verily, He hath appeared, and hath spoken in Truth. Blessed is he who confesses and acknowledges, and woe unto every remote denier."

*The Tablet of Tajalleyat*

Revealed by Baha'u'llah, at Akka.
Translated by Ali Kuli Khan.

"As to the meaning of the Cause of Baha'u'llah: know that whatever there is which has to do with the Universal Good, is divine—and whatever is divine is, certainly, for the universal good. If it is true, it is for all; if not, it is for no one. Therefore a Divine Cause of Universal Good cannot be limited either to the East or to the West; for the radiance of the Sun of Truth illumines both the East and the West, and it makes its heat felt in the South as in the North; there is no difference between one pole and the other."

*From The Tablet of Ishraket Baha'u'llah*

# SOME HIDDEN WORDS AND WORDS OF WISDOM

FROM "THE SUPREME PEN" OF BAHA'U'LLAH [7]

HE is the Glory of the Most Glorious!

This is that which descended from the Source of Majesty, through the tongue of Power and Strength, upon the prophets of the past.

We have taken its essence and clothed it with the garment of brevity, as a favour to the beloved; that they may fulfil the Covenant of God; that they may perform in themselves that which He has entrusted to them, and attain the victory by virtue of devotion in the land of the Spirit.

## OF THE LIGHT

O Son of Existence! My lamp thou art, and My Light is in thee. Therefore be illumined by it, and seek no one but Me; for I have created thee rich, and upon thee have I showered abundant grace.

By the Hands of Power I have made thee, and by the Fingers of Strength have I created thee. I have placed in thee the essence of My Light.

---

[7] From the Arabic, and Persian. Mirza Ameen U. Fareed.

Therefore depend upon It, and upon nothing else, for My Action is perfect and My Command has effect. Doubt this not, and have no uncertainty therein.

O Son of Light! Forget all else save Me, and be comforted by My Spirit. This is from the essence of My Command; therefore direct thyself to it.

Thou art My Possession, and My Possession shall never be destroyed. Why art thou in fear of thy destruction?

Thou art My Light, and My Light shall never become extinct. Why dost thou dread extinction?

Thou art My Glory, and My Glory shall not be veiled. Thou art My Garment, and My Garment shall never be outworn. Therefore abide in thy love to Me, that thou mayest find Me in the Highest Horizon.

My Right to thee is great and cannot be denied. My Mercy for thee is ample and cannot be ignored. My Love in thee exists and cannot be concealed. My Light to thee is manifest and cannot be obscured.

O Son of Spirit! The Gospel of Light I herald to thee; rejoice in it. And to the state of Holiness I call thee; Abide in it, that thou mayest be in peace for ever and ever.

O Son of Man! Magnify My Command, that I may reveal to thee the secrets of greatness and illumine thee with the Light of Eternity.

O Son of Man! My Calamity is My Providence. In appearance it is fire and vengeance; in reality it is Light and Mercy. Therefore approach it, that thou mayest become an Eternal Light and an Immortal Spirit. This is My Command; know thou It.

O Son of Man! Days have passed by thee, and thou hast occupied thyself with thy fanciful imaginations. How long wilt thou thus sleep upon thy bed? Lift up thy head from slumber, for the sun has climbed to the zenith that He may illumine thee with the Lights of Beauty.

The Light has shone upon thee from the horizon of the Mount, and the Spirit of Purity has breathed in the Sinai of thy heart.

Therefore empty thyself of doubts and fancies; then enter into this Mansion, that thou mayest be prepared for the Eternal Life and ready to meet Me. Herein there is no death, no trouble nor burden.

O Children of Men! Do ye know why We have created ye from one clay? That no one should glorify himself over the other. Be ye ever mindful of how ye were created.

Since We created ye all from the same substance, ye must be as one soul, walking with the same feet, eating with one mouth, and living in one land, that ye may manifest with your being, and by your deeds and actions, the signs of unity and the spirit of Oneness.

This is My Counsel to ye, O People of Light! Therefore follow it, that ye may attain the fruits of Holiness from the Tree of Might and Power.

O Son of Man! On the tablet of the Spirit write all We have uttered to thee, with the ink of Light; and, if thou canst not do this, then make the ink of the essence of thy heart; and, if thou art still unable, then write with the red ink shed in My Path. Verily this is more precious to Me than all else; for this Radiance shall last for ever.

O Stranger to The Friend! The candle of thy mind is lighted by the hand of My Power; extinguish it not with the contrary winds of desires and passions. The healer of all thy troubles is remembrance of Me; forget it not. Make My Love thy Capital, and cherish it as the spirit of thine eye.

O My Friends! Extinguish the lamp of ignorance, and kindle the Ever-burning Torch of guidance in the heart and mind. For in a short while the Assayers of Being shall accept naught but pure virtue in the portico of the Presence of the Adored One, and will receive none but holy deeds.

O Children of Imagination! Know ye that when the Radiant Morn dawns from the eternal horizon of Holiness, then all the Satanic secrets and deeds, which have been committed in the dark night, shall become manifest to the people of the world.

The Sun of Truth is the Word of God, upon which depends the training of the people of the country of thought.

It is the Spirit of Reality and the Water of Life. All things owe their existence to it. Its manifestation is ever according to the capacity and colouring of the mirror which reflects it. For example: Its Light, when cast on the mirrors of the wise, gives expression to wisdom; when reflected from the minds of artists, it produces manifestations of new and beautiful arts; when it shines through the minds of students, it reveals knowledge and unfolds mysteries.

All things of the world arise through man and are manifest in him, through whom they find life and development; and man is dependent for his (Spiritual) existence upon the Sun of the Word of God.

All the good names and lofty qualities are of the Word. The Word is the Fire of God, which, glowing in the hearts of people, burns away all things that are not of God. The minds of the Lovers of Light are ever aflame with this fire. It is the essence of water, which has manifested itself in the form of fire.

Outwardly it is the burning fire, while inwardly it is calm light. This is the water which giveth life to all things.

We beg of God that we may partake of this Life-giving Water of Heaven, and quaff from the Spiritual Chalice of Rest, and thus be free from all that tends to withhold us from approaching His love.

In this day he who seeks the Light of the Sun of Truth must free his mind from the tales of the past, must adorn his head with the crown of severance, and his temple with the drapery of virtue. Then shall he arrive at the ocean of Oneness and enter the presence of singleness.

The heart must become free from the fire of superstitions, that it may receive the Light of Assurance, and that it may perceive the Glory of God.

The people of Baha must serve the Lord with wisdom, teach others by their lives, and manifest the Light of God in their deeds. The effect of deeds is in truth more powerful than that of words.

## OF DIVINE HUMANITY

O Son of Man! In My Ancient Entity and in My Eternal Being, was I hidden. I knew My Love in thee, therefore I created thee; upon thee I laid My Image, and to thee revealed My Beauty.

O Son of Man! I loved thy creation, therefore I created thee. Wherefore love Me, that I may acknowledge thee, and in the Spirit of Life confirm thee.

O Son of Existence! Thy paradise is My Love; thy heaven is My Nearness; therefore enter thou and tarry not. This was ordained for thee from Our Supreme Kingdom and exalted Majesty.

O Son of Humanity! If thou lowest Me, turn away from

thyself; if My Will thou seekest, regard not thine own; that thou mayest die in Me and I live in thee.

O Son of Perception! My Fort thou art. Enter in that thou mayest be safe. My Love is in thee. Seek, and thou wilt find Me near.

O Son of Spirit! I have created thee rich! Why dost thou make thyself poor? Noble have I made thee! Why dost thou degrade thyself? Of the essence of knowledge have I manifested thee! Why searchest thou for another than Me? From the clay of Love I have kneaded thee! Why seekest thou another?

Turn thy sight unto thyself, that thou mayest find Me standing within thee, Powerful, Mighty, and Supreme.

O Son of Perception! Look thou to My Face and turn from all save Me; for My Authority is eternal and shall never cease; My Kingdom is lasting and shall not be overthrown.

If thou seekest another than Me; yea, if thou searchest the universe for evermore, yet shall thy search be in vain.

O Son of the Highest Sight! I have placed within thee a spirit from Me, that thou mightest be My Lover! Why hast thou forsaken Me and sought to love another?

O Son of Spirit! I created thee sublime, but thou hast degraded thyself. Therefore ascend to that for which thou wart created.

O Son of Man! Clothe thyself with My Beautiful Garment; and forfeit not thy portion from My Living Fountain, that thou mayest not thirst for ever.

O Son of Existence! Remember Me in My earth, that I may remember thee in My Heaven thus may our eyes delight therein.

O Son of the Throne! Thy hearing is My Hearing; hear thou with it. Thy sight is My Sight; see thou with it.

Thus mayest thou attest within thyself My Holiness; that I may attest within Myself a place of Exaltation for thee.

O Son of Humanity! The temple of being is My Throne! Purge it of everything, that I may descend therein to reign over it.

O Son of Existence! Thy heart is My Home; purify it for My Descent. Thy spirit is My Outlook; prepare it for My Manifestation.

O Son of Man! Put thy hand into My Treasury! Then will I lift My Head radiant above thy treasures.

O Son of Man! My Greatness is My Bounty to thee. My Majesty is My Mercy to thee; but that which is due to Me none can realise or comprehend. Verily I have treasured it in the stores of My Secrets, in the treasury of My Command;—as a favour to My servants and a mercy to My people.

O Children of the Spirit! Ye are My treasures, for in ye have I treasured the pearls of My Mysteries and the gems of My Knowledge.

O Son of Him who stood by His Own Entity in the Kingdom of Himself! Know that I have sent unto thee the fragrances of Holiness, have accomplished the Word in thee, have fulfilled the Bounty through thee, and have willed for thee what I have willed for Myself. Therefore be content in Me and thankful to Me.

## OF JUSTICE

Justice is loved above all. Neglect it not, if thou desirest Me.

By it thou wilt be strengthened to perceive things with thine own eyes and not by the eyes of men; to know them by thine own knowledge and not by the knowledge of any in the world. Meditate on this how thou oughtest to be.

Justice is of My Bounty to thee and of My Providence over thee; therefore, keep it ever before thy sight.

O Son of Man! Wert thou to observe Mercy, thou wouldest not regard thine own interest, but the interest of mankind. Wert thou to observe Justice. choose thou for others what thou choosest for thyself.

Know verily that he who exhorts men to equity and himself does injustice, is not of Me, though he may bear My Name.

Attribute not to any soul that which thou desirest not to be attributed to thyself, and do not promise that which thou dost not fulfil. This is My Command to thee; obey it.

The Source of all these utterances is Justice. It is the freedom of man from superstition, and imitation, that he may discern the Manifestations of God with the eye of Oneness, and consider all affairs with keen sight.

## OF DISPUTATION AND FAULT-FINDING

Verily I say the most negligent of the servants is he who disputes and prefers himself to his brother.

Purge thy mind from malice and, free from envy, enter the presence of Unity.

The tongue is especially for the mention of Me; stain it not with slander. If the fire of self overcome ye, be mindful to remember your own faults, and speak not evil of My creatures; because each one of ye is more conscious and better informed of his own self than of My creatures.

Hear no evil, and see no evil; degrade not thyself, nor lament. That is: speak no evil, that thou mayest not hear it. Think not the faults of others to be great, that thine own may not seem great. Approve not the abasement of any soul, that thine own abasement may not be exposed. Then, with stainless mind, holy heart, sanctified breast and pure thoughts, thou mayest be free during all the days of thy life, which are counted less than an instant, and with freedom may return from this mortal body to the paradise of Inner Significances and abide in the Immortal Kingdom.

Why hast thou overlooked thine own faults, and art observing defects in My servants? Whosoever does this is condemned by Me.

Breathe not the sins of any one as long as thou art a sinner. If thou doest contrary to this command, thou art not of Me. To this I bear witness.

## OF POVERTY AND WEALTH

Boast not of thine own glory over the poor; for I walk before him, and I see thee in thy miserable condition and ever grieve for thee.

If thou encounter poverty, grieve not; for, in the Time, the King of Riches will descend to thee. Fear not humility, for glory shall be thy portion.

Be not engrossed with this world, for with fire We test the gold, and with gold We try the servants.

Thou desirest gold, and We desire the separation from it. Thou hast realised therein the riches of thyself, while I realise thy wealth to consist in thy freedom from it. By My Life! This is My Knowledge, while that is thine imagining; how can My Thought agree with Thine?

Distribute My possessions among My poor, that in Heaven thou mayest receive from the boundless treasures of Glory and from the stores of Eternal Bliss.

Let the rich learn the midnight sighing of the poor, lest negligence destroy them and they be deprived of their portion of the tree of wealth.

Giving and generosity are qualities of Mine. Happy is he who adorns himself with My Virtues.

Greed must be abandoned, that thou mayest find content; for the greedy has ever been deprived, while the contented has ever been loved and esteemed.

Let not poverty trouble thee, nor rest assured in wealth. All poverty is succeeded by wealth, and all wealth is followed by poverty.

To be poor in all save God is a great blessing; make it not small, for, in the end, it will make thee rich in God.

Know ye that wealth is a strong barrier between the seeker and the Desired One, between the lover and the Beloved. Never shall the rich arrive at the abode of Nearness, nor enter into the city of contentment and resignation; save only a few.

God is the state of that wealthy one, whose wealth preventeth him not from the Everlasting Kingdom, and depriveth him not of the Eternal Possessions.

Verily, I declare by the Greatest Name, that the light of

that wealthy one shall illumine the people of Heaven, as the sun shines upon the people of the earth.

O ye who are wealthy on earth! The poor among ye are My Trust. Therefore guard My Trust, and be not wholly occupied with your own ease.

Purge thyself from the dross of wealth, and, with perfect peace, step into the paradise of poverty; thus shalt thou drink the; wine of Immortality from the fountain of death.

Rejoice not if fortune smile upon thee, and if humility overtake thee;—mourn not because of it; for, in their time, they both shall cease and be no more.

Wert thou to see the Immortal Kingdom, verily thou wouldest abandon the mortal possessions of earth; yet there is a wisdom in the former being concealed and in the latter being manifest; and this is known only to hearts that are pure.

## OF WORK AND FRUITFULNESS

Ye are the trees of My Garden; ye must bear fresh and beautiful fruits, that ye and others may be profited by them. Therefore it is necessary for ye to engage in arts and business.

This, O possessors of intellect, is the means of attaining wealth. Affairs depend upon means, and the blessing of God will appear therein and will enrich ye. Fruitless trees have been and will be only fit for fire.

O My Servant! The lowest of men are those who bear no fruit upon the earth; they are indeed counted as dead. Nay, the dead are preferred in the Presence of God before those who are indolent and negligent.

O My Servant! The best of people are they who gain by work, and spend for themselves and their kindred in the love of God, the Lord of the creatures.

The principle of faith is to lessen words and to increase deeds. He whose words exceed his acts, know verily, that his non-being is better than his being, and death better than his life.

## OF OBEDIENCE

The principle of religion is to acknowledge what is revealed by God, and to obey the laws established in His Book.

The source of all good is trust in God, obedience to His Command, and satisfaction in His Will,

O Son of Existence! Keep My Commands for love of Me, and deny thyself thine own desires if thou wishest My Pleasure.

Neglect not My Laws if thou lowest My Beauty; and forget not My Counsels if thou art hopeful to attain My Will.

O Son of Man! If thou run through all immensity and speed through the space of Heaven, thou shalt find no rest save in obedience to Our Command and in devotion before Our Face.

Magnify My Command that I may reveal to thee the secrets of greatness and illumine thee with the Lights of Eternity.

Be submissive to Me that I may descend to thee; and serve My Cause that thou mayest be victorious in Me.

Ponder over thy condition and be thoughtful in action.

Dost thou prefer to die upon thy bed, or to be martyred in My Path upon the dust; to be a Manifestation of My Command and an expression of My Light in the Highest Paradise I Discern justly, O My Servant.

## OF PRIDE

Divest yourselves from the garment of pride; and lay aside the robe of haughtiness.

I declare by My Beauty that I have created ye all from the dust, and to dust shall I turn ye again.

O Sons of Pride! For a few days' mortal reign ye have rejected My Immortal Dominion, and are arraying yourselves in robes of scarlet and gold and boasting of this. I declare by My Beauty that I will bring ye all together under the uncoloured tent of dust, and will efface the colours of all; save those who choose My Colour, which is pure from all colour.

Verily, man is uplifted to the heaven of glory and power through Meekness; again, through Pride is he degraded to the lowest station.

## OF COMPANIONSHIP

The company of the wicked increaseth sorrow; and the fellowship of the righteous removeth the rust of the mind.

He who desires to associate with God, let him associate with His Beloved; and he who desires to hear the Word of God, let him hear the words of His chosen ones.

Walk not with the wicked and confederate not with him;

for the companionship of the wicked changeth the Light of Life into fire of remorse.

If thou seekest the attainment of the Holy Spirit, be a companion of the noble; for the righteous have quaffed from the Chalice of Immortality passed by the hand of the Cup-Bearer of Eternity, and they quicken and illumine the hearts of the dead as doth the true morn.

O Friend! In the garden of the heart plant only flowers of Love. Esteem the friendship of the just; but withdraw both mind and hand from the company of the wicked.


## OF THE BELOVED AND HIS BEAUTY

What lover seeks to dwell save in the Home of The Beloved? What seeker can repose far from the Desired One?

A sincere lover finds life in the presence of The Beloved, and dies in separation. His breast is void of patience, and his heart is beyond endurance. He forsakes a hundred thousand lives, and hastens to the Mount of The Beloved.

Only one step separates thee from the plane of Nearness and the Exalted Tree of Love. Plant the first foot, and, with the other, step into the Kingdom of Eternity and enter the Pavilion of Immortality. Then hearken to what has descended from the Sea of Glory.

Pass by the low degrees of fancy, and soar to the heights of Certainty. Open the eye of Truth, that thou mayest behold the Radiant Beauty, and say, "Blessed be God, the Most Excellent of Creators!"

Listen truly: Mortal eye shall never perceive the Everlasting Beauty; and the dead mind delights only in lifeless clay; for like sees like and has affinity with its own kind.

Be blind, that thou mayest behold My Beauty. Be deaf, that thou mayest hear My Sweet Melody and Voice. Be ignorant, that thou mayest enjoy a portion from My .Knowledge. Be poor, that thou mayest obtain an everlasting share from the sea of My Eternal Wealth.

Be blind, that is, to all save My Beauty. Be deaf, that is, to all except My Word. Be ignorant, that is, of all but My Knowledge. Thus shalt thou enter My Holy Presence with pure eyes, keen ears, and a mind undimmed.

Close one eye and open the other. Close the one to the world and all that is therein; and open the other to the Holy Beauty of The Beloved.

Be not satisfied with the beauty that is mortal; discarding the Eternal Beauty; and attach not thyself to the world of clay.

O Son of Passion! The people of wisdom and insight struggled for years, and failed to attain to the meeting of the Exalted One; while thou hast arrived at home without hastening, and hast attained the goal without searching.

Yet, after gaining these, thou wert so veiled with thyself that thine eyes did not behold the Beauty of The Beloved, and thy hand did not reach to the Hem of the Friend's garment. Marvel at this, O possessors of insight.

O My Friend by Word! Reflect a little! Hast thou ever heard of the beloved and the stranger dwelling in the same heart? Therefore, send away the stranger, so that The Beloved may enter His Home.

If thou desirest Me, desire no other than Me. If thou seekest My Beauty, withdraw thy glance from the people of the world; for My Will and the will of another are like fire and water which cannot be contained in the same mind and heart.

Break the cage, and, like unto the bird of love, soar into the atmosphere of holiness; leave the self, and rest with heavenly souls upon the sacred plain of God.

Walk ye in the path of the good pleasure of The Friend. His good pleasure is ever in His creatures. That is; a friend should not enter the home of his friend without his good pleasure, nor interfere with his possessions, nor prefer his desire to that of his friend, nor seek preference in any condition. Consider this, O ye people of thought.

Alas! Alas! O Lovers of Passion! With the swiftness of lightning ye have left the Spiritual Beloved, and to Satanic thoughts have ye attached your minds. Ye worship fancy, and call it a fact; ye are gazing at a thorn, and call it a flower.

Not an unselfish breath have ye breathed, nor hath a breeze of self-denial come from the garden of your hearts.

Ye have cast to the winds the merciful Counsels of The Beloved, have effaced them from the tablet of your minds, and have become as low animals feasting in the pastures of lust and desire.

Why are ye heedless of the remembrance of The Beloved? and why are ye far from the Presence of The Friend? The Absolute Beauty is established upon the Throne of Glory, under the Peerless Canopy; while ye are engaged in contention according to your own desire.

The fragrances of holiness are wafted, and the breezes of generosity are blowing; but ye have lost the power of scent, and are bereft of them all. Alas for you, and for them who follow in your steps and walk after your ways!

O Heedless Ones! Think not that the mysteries of hearts

are concealed; nay, rather know with certainty that they are inscribed in clear type, and are openly manifest in The Presence.

Truly, I say, all that ye have concealed in your hearts is before Us, clear, manifest and open as the day; but the cause of concealment is from Our Generosity and Mercy, not from your merit.

O Son of Man! I have shed a dew from the past Ocean of My Mercy upon the dwellers of the world, and have found none approaching; because all have attached themselves to the impure water of wine, and have left the immortal, delicate Wine of Unity; they have turned from the Chalice of the Immortal Beauty, and have been content with the mortal cup. "Evil is that with which they are contented!"

Close not thine eye to the peerless Wine of the Eternal Beloved, and open not thine eye to the turbid and mortal wine.

Take immortal cups from the hand of the Cup-bearer of Oneness, and thou shalt become all consciousness, and hear the inaudible Utterance of Reality. Say, O worthless ones! Why have ye turned from My Eternal, Holy Wine, to mortal water?

How is it that thou wilt not touch thine own garment with hands soiled by sugar; while, with thy mind soiled by the filth of passion and lust, thou seekest companionship with Me, and desirest to be directed to the dominions of My Holiness! Alas! alas! for that which ye have desired!

Thou art like a jewelled sword concealed in a dark sheath, by reason of which its value is unknown to the jewellers. Come forth from the sheath of self and desire, that thy jewels may become open and manifest before the world.

Guidance hath ever been by words, but, at this time, it is by deeds. That is; all pure deeds must appear from the temple of man, because all are partners in words, but pure and holy deeds belong especially to Our friends. Strive with your life to be distinguished among all people by deeds. Thus we exhort ye.

O Son of Desire! How long fliest thou in the atmosphere of self? I have granted thee wings that thou mightest soar in the holy atmosphere of realities, and not in the air of Satanic fancies. I favoured thee with a comb, that thou mightest comb the locks of My Head and not to wound My Throat.

The bride of wonderful Significances, who was concealed behind the veils of words, hath appeared through Divine Providence and Heavenly Bounties, like unto the radiance of the Beauty of The Beloved.

I testify, O Friends, that the Bounty has become complete, the Evidence is accomplished, the Argument manifested, and the Reason affirmed.

What will your endeavours show forth from the degrees of devotion?

The source of Love is to advance to The Beloved and to abandon all else save Him, and to have no hope save His will.

No peace is ordained for thee save by departing from thyself and coming to Me! Verily, thy glory should be in My Name, not in thy name; thy trust upon My Countenance, not upon thine own; for I will to be loved above all that is.

My Love is My Fortress. Who enters therein is rescued and safe; whoever turns away from it is led astray and perishes.

God, singly and alone, abideth in His Own Place, which is Holy above space and time, mention and utterance, sign, description and definition, height and depth.

O my God! O my God! Adorn the heads of Thy chosen ones with the crown of Love, and their temples with the garniture of virtue.

(Supplication.) O my God! Make Thy Beauty to be my food, and let Thy Presence be my drink. Let my trust be in Thy Will, and my deeds according to Thy Command.

Let my service be acceptable to Thee, and my action a praise to Thee. Let my help come only from Thee; and ordain my home to be Thy Mansion, boundless and holy.

Thou art the Precious, the Ever-Present, the Loving. O Thou, My Beloved! Grant unto me Thy Sign of Assurance to guard me from the doubts of the wandering. Thou art my Helper, the Powerful, the Mighty.


## OF KNOWLEDGE

The root of all knowledge is the knowledge of God; Glory be to Him! Knowledge is impossible save through His Manifestation.

O My Brother! Hear My Beautiful Words from My Sweet Tongue, and drink the Water of Life from the Fountain of My Lips. Sow the seeds of My Innate Wisdom in the pure ground of the heart, and water it with conviction; then the flower of My Knowledge and Wisdom shall spring up verdantly in the holy sanctuary of the heart.

Sow the seeds of knowledge and wisdom in the fertile grounds of the mind, and conceal them there until the hyacinth of Divine Wisdom springs up in the heart and not in the clay.

Drink the wine of Significancies from the Lips of the Merciful, and behold the radiance of the light of the Sun of

Explanation, without veil or cover, from the Dawning-Place of the Word of God:

Spread the seeds of My Immediate Wisdom in the fertile soil of the heart and water it with the water of certainty; thus shall the hyacinths of My Knowledge and Wisdom spring up and flourish.

The progress of man depends upon faithfulness, wisdom, chastity, intelligence, and action. He is ever degraded by ignorance, lack of faith, untruth and selfishness.

Verily, man is not called man until he be imbued with the attributes of The Merciful. He is not man because of wealth and adornment, learning and refinement. Blessed is he who is free; seeking the shore of the Sea of Purity and loving the melody of the dove of Virtue.

In this day all must serve God with purity and virtue. The effect of the word spoken by the teacher depends upon his purity of purpose. Some are content with words; but the truth of words is tested by deeds, and dependent upon life.

Deeds reveal the station of the man. The words must be according to what has proceeded from the Mouth of the Will of God.

O my God! O my God! Unite the hearts of Thy servants and reveal to them Thy Great Purpose. May they follow Thy Commandments and abide in Thy Law. Help them, O God, in their endeavour, and grant them strength to serve Thee. O God, leave them not to themselves, but guide their steps by the light of knowledge and cheer their hearts by Thy Love.

## OF ONENESS

My Eternity is My creation. I have created it for thee. My Oneness is My design. I have designed it for thee; therefore clothe thyself with it. Thus thou mayest be a star of My Omnipresence for ever.

Alas! that a hundred thousand ideal languages are spoken by One Tongue, and that a hundred thousand hidden meanings are unfolded in One Melody, and there is no ear to hearken, nor any heart to perceive a single letter!

Let the people of Certainty know that a new Garden has appeared in the Open Court of Holiness, and that all the people of the Heights, and the temples of the Exalted Heaven, are around it.

Endeavour to reach that station and discover the truths of the mystery of Love from its blossoms, and unveil abundant knowledge of the Oneness from its eternal fruits. Radiant are the eyes of him who has entered therein with trust.

O Dead Men on the Bed of Negligence! Centuries have passed, and ye have ended your precious limes; yet not a single breath of purity hath ever come from ye to Our Holy Presence. Ye are drowned in the sea of polytheism while talking of Oneness.

Oneness, in its true significance, means that God alone should be realised as the One Power which animates and dominates all things, which are but manifestations of its energy.

FROM THE BOOK OF THE COVENANT

"IN wealth fear is concealed and peril is hidden. Behold, and then reflect upon that which The Merciful One hath revealed in the Koran;—"Woe unto every maligner and backbiter who heapeth up riches and counteth them over." There is no continuance in the riches of this world; that which is subject to mortality and undergoeth a change, hath never been and is not worth regarding.

O People of the World! I enjoin ye to that which is the means of the elevation of your station. Hold to the virtue of God, and grasp the hem of that which is just.

Verily, I say the tongue is for mentioning that which is good; pollute it not with evil speech. God hath forgiven ye that which is past; hereafter ye must all speak that which is befitting; avoid execration, reviling, and that which is aggravating to man. The station of man is high.

The station of man is great, if he holds to reality and truth; and if he be firm and steadfast in the Commands. The true man appeareth before the Merciful One like unto the heavens; his sight and hearing are the sun and moon; his bright and shining qualities are the stars; his station is the highest one; his traces are the educators of existence.

Every believer who hath found the Perfume of the Garment in this day, and turneth with a pure heart towards the Supreme Horizon, he is mentioned as one of the followers of Baha on the Red Page (the Red Page means the station of martyrdom, and is the highest).

O People of the World! The Creed of God is for love and union; make it not to be a cause of discord and disunion. In the sight of the men of discernment, and those who are holding to the Manifestation, that which is the means of preservation and the cause of the ease and tranquillity of the Servants, is revealed from the Supreme Pen; but the ignorant of the earth, who are fostered in ambition and lust, are heedless of the matured Wisdom of the True Wise One, and are speaking and working in imaginations and fancies.

O Saints of God and His Loyal Ones! Kings are the

appearances of power and the daysprings of the Might and Wealth of the True One. Pray on their behalf, for the government of the earth is ordained to those souls; but the hearts He hath appointed for Himself.

He hath forbidden dispute and strife, with an absolute prohibition. This is the Command of God, in this greatest Manifestation, and He hath preserved it from any order of annulment and hath adorned it with the ornament of confirmation. Verily, He is the All-Knowing and the All-Wise.

It is incumbent upon all to aid those souls who are the daysprings of authority and the dawning-points of command, and who are adorned with the ornament of equity and justice. Blessings be upon the princes and the learned ones. These are My trusted ones amongst My Servants; these are the rising-points of My Commandments amongst My creatures. Upon them be My Glory, My Mercy, and My Grace, which have surrounded all existence.

O Servants! Make not the causes of order to be the causes of confusion, and make not the reason of union to be the occasion of dispute. This exalted Word resembles water for extinguishing the fire of hatred and animosity, which is deposited in all minds and hearts.

The different creeds will attain the Light of real Union through the simple Word. Verily, He sayeth the Truth and guideth in the Path; and He is the Powerful, the Mighty, and the Wonderful.

## TRUE BELIEF

The Guidance of God is that which will always guide people in the right way.

All human beings are earthly; their hearts are connected with this world. Day and night their thoughts and occupations are earthly; all belong to this world. They think about the honours of this world, or about the riches and wealth of this world, or of name and fame in this world. Their days and nights pass in this way.

The Guidance of God makes it evident and plain, when the Way of the Kingdom, the Divine Path, is opened; that this is the road of the Kingdom.

It is not sufficient only to distinguish the Way of the Kingdom—only to discover the Heavenly Way—you must travel upon it until the end is reached. For example;—that a man discovers the way to America is not sufficient. He must travel in it, that he may reach that country; otherwise, if he remain for years discovering more about the way, and does not travel by it, he will never arrive.

It is not sufficient for a child to know where the school is; he must study in it, that he may gain knowledge. Faith is not merely to know which is the school, and to recognise the teacher; but one must acquire knowledge in this school. If one does not gain knowledge, it is useless to know of the school.

This is what Christ said: "Ye shall know the tree by its fruits."

If you see one who is truthful, who really believes and is just, who is attracted to the kingdom, and whose will is annihilated in the Way of God; then you will know that he is a tree of the Kingdom, if he shows forth all these qualities.

If you see one whose heart is attached to this world, and in whom there is no truthfulness or detachment, or turning to God; one who is not occupied in praising and speaking of God, or in attraction to the Love of God—then you will know that he is a tree of darkness.

True belief is not only to acknowledge the Oneness of God. By belief we mean that the reality of a man will be characterised by Divine characteristics. If his reality is dark, he will become enlightened. If he is heedless he will become conscious; if he is sleeping, he will be awakened; if he is earthly, he will become heavenly; if he is Satanic, he will become Divine. This is the meaning of true belief.

Therefore, I say that man must travel in the Way of God. Day and night he must endeavour to become better; his belief must increase and become firmer; his good qualities and his turning to God must be greater; the fire of his love must flame more brightly. Then, day by day, he will make progress.

For to stop advancing is the means of going back. The bird when he flies soars ever higher and higher. All the time he endeavours to mount higher, for as soon as he stops flying he will come down.

Every day in the morning when arising, you should compare to-day with yesterday, and see in what condition you are. If you see your belief is stronger, and your heart more occupied with God, and your love increased, and your freedom from the world greater; then thank God, and ask for the increase of these qualities. You must pray and repent for all that you have done which is wrong; and you must implore and ask for help and assistance, that you may be better than yesterday; so that you may continue to make progress.

Do not let the desires of the self find a place within you; for it is certain that even when you reach the highest state of spirituality, one worldly desire can cause your downfall.

The spirit is like a bird; when it flies in the air it is always mounting; but the self is like the hunter, who is thinking how to catch the bird. You will see that by one arrow, one shot, it will be brought low.

This arrow is the connection with this world; the occupations of this world; the desires of this world; the honours of this world.

In many ways the hunter will stop the spirit from ascending. That is why you must ask and implore and entreat, "O God! protect me from myself!"

ABDUL-BAHA ABBAS

## THE COMMANDS OF THE BLESSED MASTER
## ABDUL-BAHA

AS REVEALED IN TABLETS AND INSTRUCTIONS FOR THE BELOVED IN AMERICA

"To live the life.

To be no cause of grief to any one.

To love each other fully.

To be kind to all people and to love them with a pure spirit.

Should opposition or injury happen, we must bear it and be kind, and, through all, we must love the people. Should calamity exist in the greatest degree, we must rejoice, for these things are the Gifts and Favours of God.

To be silent concerning the faults of others; to pray for them; and help them, through kindness, to correct their faults.

To look always at the good and not at the bad. If a man has ten good qualities and one bad one, we must look at the ten and forget the one. And if a man has ten bad qualities and one good one, we must look at the one and forget the ten.

To never allow ourselves to speak one unkind word about another; even though that other be our enemy. To rebuke those who speak to us of the faults of others.

All of our deeds must be done in kindness.

To be occupied in spreading the Teachings; for only through obedience to this Command, our Master has said, will we receive the power and confirmation of the Spirit; and that whosoever is granted this power and confirmation of the Spirit, is under the Favour of God; but, otherwise, he is as a lamp without light. The Master has also said that 'Every seed cast in this great and magnificent period will be cultivated by God, and produce plants, through the abundance of the clouds of His Mercy.'

To cut our hearts from ourselves and from the world.

To be humble.

To be servants of each other, and to know that we are less than any one else.

To be as one soul in many bodies; for the more we love each other the nearer we shall be to God; but that our love, our unity, our obedience, must not be by confession but of reality.

To act with caution and wisdom.

To be truthful.

To be hospitable.

To be reverent.

To be a cause of healing for every sick one; a comforter for every sorrowful one; a pleasant water for every thirsty one; a Heavenly Table for every hungry one; a guide for every seeker; rain for cultivation; a star to every . horizon; a light for every lamp; a herald to every yearning one for the Kingdom of God.

Our Blessed Master said:

'By these things you know the faithful servant of God.'"